Learning AWS IoT

Effectively manage connected devices on the AWS cloud using services such as AWS Greengrass, AWS button, predictive analytics and machine learning

Agus Kurniawan

BIRMINGHAM - MUMBAI

Learning AWS IoT

Commissioning Editor: Gebin George
Acquisition Editor: Heramb Bhavsar
Content Development Editor: Abhishek Jadhav
Technical Editor: Swathy Mohan
Copy Editors: Safis Editing, Dipti Mankame
Project Coordinator: Judie Jose
Proofreader: Safis Editing
Indexer: Rekha Nair
Graphics: Tom Scaria
Production Coordinator: Nilesh Mohite

First published: January 2018

Production reference: 1250118

Published by Packt Publishing Ltd.
Livery Place
35 Livery Street
Birmingham
B3 2PB, UK.

ISBN 978-1-78839-611-0

www.packtpub.com

`mapt.io`

Mapt is an online digital library that gives you full access to over 5,000 books and videos, as well as industry leading tools to help you plan your personal development and advance your career. For more information, please visit our website.

Why subscribe?

- Spend less time learning and more time coding with practical eBooks and Videos from over 4,000 industry professionals

- Improve your learning with Skill Plans built especially for you

- Get a free eBook or video every month

- Mapt is fully searchable

- Copy and paste, print, and bookmark content

PacktPub.com

Did you know that Packt offers eBook versions of every book published, with PDF and ePub files available? You can upgrade to the eBook version at `www.PacktPub.com` and as a print book customer, you are entitled to a discount on the eBook copy. Get in touch with us at `service@packtpub.com` for more details.

At `www.PacktPub.com`, you can also read a collection of free technical articles, sign up for a range of free newsletters, and receive exclusive discounts and offers on Packt books and eBooks.

Contributors

About the author

Agus Kurniawan is a lecturer, researcher, IT consultant, and author. He has more than 16 years of experience in various software and hardware development projects for various companies. He also has been delivering materials in training and workshops, and delivering technical writing. He has been awarded the Microsoft Most Valuable Professional (MVP) award for 13 years in a row. He is currently doing some research related to software engineering, machine learning, networking and security systems at the Faculty of Computer Science, University of Indonesia, Indonesia.

> *I would like to thank the Amazon AWS and IoT communities anywhere in the world for contributing and making learning AWS IoT easy. Last, a thank you to my wife, Ela and my children, Thariq and Zahra for their great supports to complete this book.*

About the reviewer

Ruben Oliva Ramos is a computer systems engineer from Tecnologico of León Institute, with a master's degree in computer and electronics systems engineering, with a specialization in teleinformatics and networking from University of Salle Bajio in Leon, Guanajuato, Mexico. He has more than 5 years of experience of developing web applications to control and monitor devices connected with Arduino and Raspberry Pi using web frameworks and cloud services to build the IoT applications.

I would like to thank my lord, Jesus Christ for giving me strength and courage to pursue this project; to my dearest wife, Mayte; our two lovely sons, Ruben and Dario; to my father (Ruben); my dearest mom (Rosalia); my brother (Juan Tomas); and my sister (Rosalia), whom I love, for all their support while reviewing this book, for allowing me to pursue my dream, and tolerating me not being with them because of my busy job.

Packt is searching for authors like you

If you're interested in becoming an author for Packt, please visit `authors.packtpub.com` and apply today. We have worked with thousands of developers and tech professionals, just like you, to help them share their insight with the global tech community. You can make a general application, apply for a specific hot topic that we are recruiting an author for, or submit your own idea.

Table of Contents

Preface

The Internet of Things (IoT) market has increased a lot in the past few years, and the adoption and development of IoT have an upward trend. Analysis and predictions say that enterprise IoT platforms are the future of IoT. AWS IoT is currently leading the market with its wide range of device support SDKs and its versatile management console.

This book initially introduces you to the IoT platforms and how they make our IoT development easy. It then covers the complete AWS IoT suite and how it can be used to develop secure communication between internet-connected things, such as sensors, actuators, embedded devices, and smart applications. The book also covers the various modules of AWS—AWS Greengrass, AWS device SDKs, AWS IoT Platform, AWS Button, AWS Management consoles, AWS-related CLI, and API references, all with practical use cases.

Toward the end, the book supplies security-related best practices in order to make bidirectional communication more secure. When you've finished this book, you'll be up and running with the AWS IoT suite and building IoT projects.

Who this book is for

This book is for anyone who wants to get started with the AWS IoT suite and implement it with practical use cases. This book acts as an extensive guide, on completion of which you will be in a position to start building IoT projects using the AWS IoT platform and start using cloud services for your projects.

What this book covers

Chapter 1, *Getting Started with AWS IoT*, introduces the book and presents the platforms, hardware, and tools that will be used, getting started to use AWS IoT.

Chapter 2, *Connecting IoT Devices to AWS IoT Platform*, will show you how to build an IoT application that involves the AWS IoT platform.

Chapter 3, *Optimizing IoT Computing Using AWS Greengrass*, walks through how to deploy AWS Greengrass on local IoT devices to enable customers to build IoT devices that can execute local applications.

Chapter 4, *Building Local AWS Lambda with AWS Greengrass*, will teach the reader how to deploy local AWS Lambda with AWS Greengrass to enable IoT devices use a local AWS server.

Chapter 5, *Expanding IoT Capabilities with AWS IoT Button,* will show how to work with AWS IoT button and integrate it with their IoT projects.

Chapter 6, *Visualizing AWS IoT Data,* will build IoT data visualizations that are obtained from IoT devices.

Chapter 7, *Building Predictive Analytics for AWS IoT,* will explain how to manage AWS IoT data and make predictive analytics to get insight from data.

Chapter 8, *Securing AWS IoT,* will show how to secure AWS IoT between AWS IoT servers and IoT devices.

To get the most out of this book

As the practical examples involve the use of AWS, an AWS account is required. The hardware requirements for this book include the following:

- Raspberry Pi 3
- Arduino Yún
- AWS IoT Button
- SimpleLink™ Wi-Fi® CC3220SF Wireless LaunchPad
- DHT22 Sensor
- LEDs
- Breadboard
- Jumper cables

The software requirements are as follows:

- AWS License
- Arduino Software
- Python and its libraries
- Node.js

Download the example code files

You can download the example code files for this book from your account at `www.packtpub.com`. If you purchased this book elsewhere, you can visit `www.packtpub.com/support` and register to have the files emailed directly to you.

You can download the code files by following these steps:

1. Log in or register at `www.packtpub.com`.
2. Select the **SUPPORT** tab.
3. Click on **Code Downloads & Errata**.
4. Enter the name of the book in the **Search** box and follow the onscreen instructions.

Once the file is downloaded, please make sure that you unzip or extract the folder using the latest version of:

- WinRAR/7-Zip for Windows
- Zipeg/iZip/UnRarX for Mac
- 7-Zip/PeaZip for Linux

The code bundle for the book is also hosted on GitHub at `https://github.com/PacktPublishing/Learning-AWS-IoT`. We also have other code bundles from our rich catalog of books and videos available at `https://github.com/PacktPublishing/`. Check them out!

Download the color images

We also provide a PDF file that has color images of the screenshots/diagrams used in this book. You can download it from `http://www.packtpub.com/sites/default/files/downloads/LearningAWSIoT.pdf`.

Conventions used

There are a number of text conventions used throughout this book.

`CodeInText`: Indicates code words in text, database table names, folder names, filenames, file extensions, pathnames, dummy URLs, user input, and Twitter handles. Here is an example: "To install the AWS IoT SDK for JavaScript, you can do so through the `npm` package."

A block of code is set as follows:

```
device
  .on('connect', function() {
    console.log('connected');
    device.subscribe('topic_1');
    device.publish('topic_1', JSON.stringify({ test_data: 1}));
  });
```

When we wish to draw your attention to a particular part of a code block, the relevant lines or items are set in bold:

```
device
  .on('message', function(topic, payload) {
  console.log('recv:', topic, payload.toString());
});

console.log('Sensor subscriber started.');
```

Any command-line input or output is written as follows:

```
$ npm install aws-iot-device-sdk
```

Bold: Indicates a new term, an important word, or words that you see onscreen. For example, words in menus or dialog boxes appear in the text like this. Here is an example: "You can click on the **Get started** button in the **Configuring a device** section".

Warnings or important notes appear like this.

Tips and tricks appear like this.

Get in touch

Feedback from our readers is always welcome.

General feedback: Email feedback@packtpub.com and mention the book title in the subject of your message. If you have questions about any aspect of this book, please email us at questions@packtpub.com.

Errata: Although we have taken every care to ensure the accuracy of our content, mistakes do happen. If you have found a mistake in this book, we would be grateful if you would report this to us. Please visit www.packtpub.com/submit-errata, selecting your book, clicking on the Errata Submission Form link, and entering the details.

Piracy: If you come across any illegal copies of our works in any form on the Internet, we would be grateful if you would provide us with the location address or website name. Please contact us at copyright@packtpub.com with a link to the material.

If you are interested in becoming an author: If there is a topic that you have expertise in and you are interested in either writing or contributing to a book, please visit authors.packtpub.com.

Reviews

Please leave a review. Once you have read and used this book, why not leave a review on the site that you purchased it from? Potential readers can then see and use your unbiased opinion to make purchase decisions, we at Packt can understand what you think about our products, and our authors can see your feedback on their book. Thank you!

For more information about Packt, please visit packtpub.com.

1
Getting Started with AWS IoT

Deploying multiple **Internet of things (IoT)** devices on some locations and serving all requests from IoT devices needs more attention in order to obtain high availability and good performance. One of the approaches is to deploy a cloud server with high availability and advanced features. In this chapter, we will get started working with **Amazon Web Services (AWS)** IoT.

By the end of this chapter, you will know how to:

- Introduce AWS IoT
- Introduce IoT devices and platform for AWS IoT
- Use AWS IoT Management Console
- Use AWS IoT device SDK
- Set up AWS IoT for your IoT project
- Build a program to access AWS IoT

So, let's get started!

Introducing AWS IoT

In recent years, there have been a lot of IoT boards built by either manufacturers or indie makers. Each IoT offers unique features to build IoT applications to address users problems. Sensor and actuator devices are attached to these IoT boards to generate data. There is a lot of sensor data from IoT devices that we can analyze.

Suppose we have various IoT boards that are deployed on some locations. Since these IoT devices generate sensor data, we need a backend server with high availability to serve incoming data. In particular cases, we also need to analyze the data to obtain insights. To perform this scenario, we need more computing engines, such as storage and machine learning engines.

The general design of AWS IoT architecture is illustrated in the following figure. There are several components inside AWS IoT, including its endpoints. IoT devices can access AWS IoT through the AWS message broker with their own SDK. AWS IoT also provides SDK for various IoT device platforms. Using AWS IoT SDK, IoT devices can access AWS IoT directly. We will review some AWS IoT SDK, including its protocol and API, throughout this book. The AWS IoT components are shown in the following image:

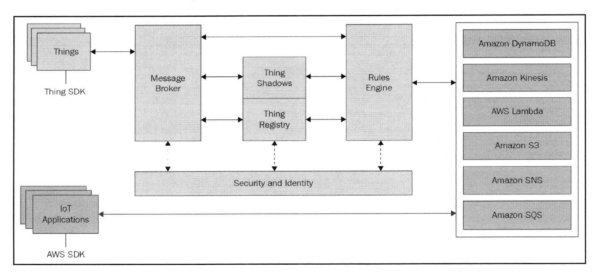

From the preceding figure, we can see the following AWS IoT components:

- **Message broker**: This is basically an AWS IoT endpoint where IoT devices can access the AWS server through the **Message Queuing Telemetry Transport (MQTT)** protocol. Message broker also supports primitive protocols, such as the HTTP protocol. Your IoT device can send data with AWS IoT through HTTP REST.

- **Thing Registry**: This manages all the IoT device administration. You can register and configure your IoT devices, including configuring certificates and IoT device IDs.
- **Thing Shadows**: This refers to a device shadow that has functionalities to keep the current state information for a specific thing in a JSON document.
- **Rules Engine**: This provides message processing and integration with other AWS services. If you have deployed AWS services, you can apply a rule engine on those services.

Some AWS IoT components will be explored in this book.

Introducing IoT devices and platforms for AWS IoT

The IoT platform can connect to an internet network and interact with other platforms. Generally speaking, talking about the IoT in terms of a device platform is a huge topic. In this section, we review some IoT platforms that interact with AWS IoT.

Technically, we can describe a connectivity model between IoT devices and the AWS IoT backend. We can categorize the IoT device platform into three models based on their supported connectivity. For an IoT device with network capabilities, if this device has support for all the required AWS IoT devices, then this device can access AWS IoT directly.

Several IoT devices probably have network capabilities, but their supported protocols are not covered by AWS IoT. For this scenario, we need to build a gateway that serves and translates the IoT device protocol to the AWS IoT protocol. This gateway provides some network capabilities, such as Bluetooth, Wi-Fi, XBee, and other RF, in order to serve all exchange of data among IoT devices and AWS IoT servers.

Finally, IoT devices without network capabilities still have a chance to communicate with AWS IoT. There are two methods that we can implement for this scenario. If the IoT device can extend its functionality, we can add a network module with the supported AWS IoT protocol. Another option is to connect this IoT device to a computer. Since a computer usually has capabilities to connect to an external network, we can build a program as a bridge between the IoT device and the AWS IoT backend. The program will interact with the IoT device, for example, by sensing and actuating, and perform a data exchange with the AWS IoT backend.

All the connectivity scenarios that we have so far discussed are illustrated in the following figure:

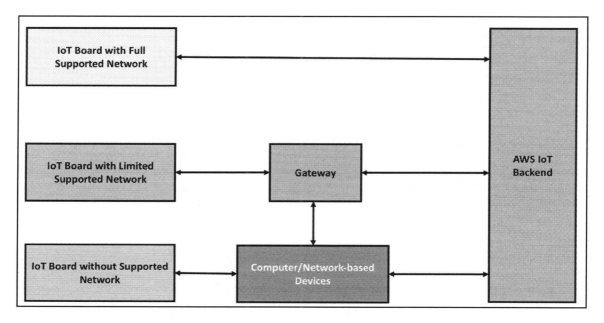

In the following section, we will explore several IoT device platforms that are widely used on the customer side to communicate with AWS IoT. Amazon also provides a list of AWS IoT starter kits from Amazon partners at `https://aws.amazon.com/iot-platform/getting-started/#kits`. We will review some devices with the supported AWS IoT platform.

Arduino

Arduino is a widely used development board. This board is well-known in the embedded community. Mostly, Arduino boards are built using Atmel AVR, but some boards use other **Microcontroller Units** (**MCUs**) depending on who is in joint venture with Arduino. Currently, Arduino boards are built by Arduino.

We will review several Arduino boards from Arduino.cc (`https://www.arduino.cc/en/Main/Products`). We can read a comparison of all the Arduino boards by visiting `http://www.arduino.cc/en/Products/Compare`. We will review some Arduino boards, such as Arduino Uno, Arduino 101, and Arduino MKR1000:

- The **Arduino Uno** model is widely used in Arduino development. It's built on top of MCU ATmega328P. The board provides several digital and analog I/O pins, which we can attach our sensor and actuator devices to. SPI and I2C protocols are also provided by Arduino Uno.

  For further information about the board, I recommend you read the board specification at `http://www.arduino.cc/en/Main/ArduinoBoardUno`. The Arduino board is shown in the following image:

  Since Arduino Uno does not provide network modules, either Ethernet or wireless modules, we should put the network module with the supported AWS IoT to enable it to communicate with other machines.

- **Arduino 101** is the same model as Arduino Uno in terms of I/O pins. Arduino 101 runs Intel® Curie™ as its core module. For more information, refer to `http://www.intel.com/content/www/us/en/wearables/wearable-soc.html`. This board has a built-in Bluetooth module. If you want Arduino 101 work with a Wi-Fi network, you should add an additional Wi-Fi shield. I recommend using Arduino Wi-Fi Shield 101. For more information, refer to `https://store.arduino.cc/genuino-101`:

- **Arduino Yún** is a microcontroller board based on the ATmega32u4 and the Atheros AR9331. This board runs OpenWrt Linux, called **LininoOS**. Arduino Yún can connect through Ethernet and Wi-Fi modules that are built-in features on the board. For further information on Arduino Yún, you can visit `https://store.arduino.cc/arduino-yun`. You can see a form of Arduino Yún in the following image:

Arduino also provides another model with a small factor. It's **Arduino Yún Mini**. For more information, refer to `https://store.arduino.cc/arduino-yun-mini`. This board removes the Ethernet socket from the body to give a smaller board size. You can see Arduino Yún Mini in the following image:

Raspberry Pi

The Raspberry Pi is a low-cost credit-card sized computer, created by Eben Upton. It's a mini computer for educational purposes. To see all Raspberry Pi models, you can refer to `https://www.raspberrypi.org/products/`. Raspberry Pi 3 Model B and Raspberry Pi Zero are described here:

- **Raspberry Pi 3 Model B**: This is the third-generation Raspberry Pi. This board consists of a Quad-Core 64-bit CPU, Wi-Fi, and Bluetooth. It's recommended for your IoT solution:

- **Raspberry Pi Zero**: This is a small computer, half the size of model A+. It runs with a single-core CPU and no network module, but it provides micro HDMI to be connected to a monitor. Since there is no network module in Raspberry Pi Zero, you can extend it by adding a module; for instance, Ethernet USB or Wi-Fi USB to connect to a network. You can see a form of Raspberry Pi Zero in the following image:

BeagleBone Black and Green

BeagleBone Black (BBB) Rev.C is a development kit based on an AM335x processor, which integrates an ARM Cortex™-A8 core operating at up to 1 GHz. BBB is more powerful than Raspberry Pi. The BBB board also provides internal 4 GB 8-bit eMMC onboard flash storage.

BBB supports several OS, such as Debian, Android, and Ubuntu. For more information on BBB, refer to `https://beagleboard.org/black`:

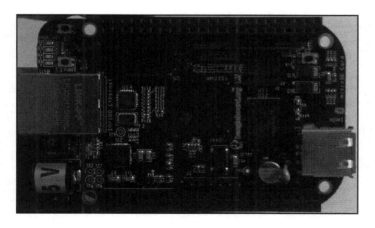

SeeedStudio **BeagleBone Green** (**BBG**) is a joint effort by BeagleBoard.org and Seeed Studio. BBG has the same features as BBB, although theHDMI port is replaced by Grove connectors, so the BBG price is lower than BBB. You can find out more and buy this board at http://www.seeedstudio.com/depot/SeeedStudio-BeagleBone-Green-p-2504.html:

IoT boards based on ESP8266 MCU

ESP8266 is a low-cost Wi-Fi MCU with full TCP/IP support. It's built by Espressif, a Chinese manufacturer. For further information about this chip, refer to http://espressif.com/en/products/hardware/esp8266ex/overview.

There are many boards based on the ESP8266 chip. The following is a list of board platforms built on top of ESP8266 MCU:

- **NodeMCU**: This board uses NodeMCU firmware, with Lua as the programming language. For more information, refer to the official website at http://www.nodemcu.com/index_en.html.
- **SparkFun ESP8266 Thing**: This is developed by SparkFun. You should use serial hardware, such as FTDI, to write a program in this board, but this product is ready for a LiPo charger. You can read more about it at https://www.sparkfun.com/products/13231.

- **SparkFun ESP8266 Thing – Dev**: This board already includes a FTDI-to-USB tool, but no LiPo charger. It's developed by SparkFun and product information can be found at `https://www.sparkfun.com/products/13711`.
- **SparkFun Blynk Board – ESP8266**: This board includes temperature and humidity sensor devices. You can read about it at `https://www.sparkfun.com/products/13794`.
- **Adafruit HUZZAH with ESP8266 WiFi**: This is developed by Adafruit. Product information can be found at `https://www.adafruit.com/products/2821`.

If you're interested in the ESP8266 chip, I recommend that you join the ESP8266 forum at `http://www.esp8266.com`.

Although NodeMCU v2 and SparkFun ESP8266 Thing boards have the same chip, their chip model is different. NodeMCU v2 uses the ESP8266 module. On the other hand, the SparkFun ESP8266 Thing board uses the ESP8266EX chip. In addition, the SparkFun ESP8266 Thing board provides a LiPo connector, which you can attach to an external battery:

IoT boards based on ESP32

ESP32 is a chip that has two network stacks, Wi-Fi and BLE from Espressif, and is available at http://espressif.com/en/products/hardware/esp32/overview. This chip enables you to connect servers through a built-in Wi-Fi module. Based on my experience, there are a lot of IoT boards based on the ESP32 chip. The following is a list of ESP32 development boards:

- **SparkFun ESP32 Thing**, available at https://www.sparkfun.com/products/13907
- **Espressif ESP32 Development Board**, available at https://www.adafruit.com/product/3269

You also find various IoT boards based on the ESP32 chip at Aliexpress or online stores. A form of SparkFun ESP32 Thing is shown in the following image:

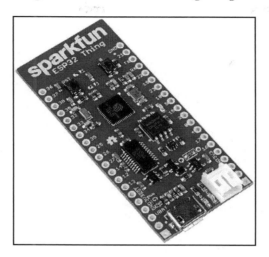

We can also use Mongoose OS ESP32-DevKitC from Cesanta to build applications for AWS IoT. To communicate with AWS IoT, they provide the Mongoose OS, which runs on ESP32. Several libraries from the Mongoose OS can be used to communicate with AWS IoT. The Mongoose OS ESP32-DevKitC from Cesanta is shown in the image source https://mongoose-os.com/aws-iot-starter-kit/.

IoT boards based on TI CC32XX MCU

TI CC3200 is a Wi-Fi MCU from **Texas Instruments** (**TI**). The new version of TI CC3200 is TI CC3220. This chip is based on ARM Cortex-M4 from TI. This board is a complete solution for IoT. This chip is supported for station, **Access Point** (**AP**), and Wi-Fi Direct modes. Regarding security, TI CC32XX supports WPA2 personal and enterprise security and **Web Processing Service** (**WPS**) 2.0. A comparison of TI CC3200 and TI CC3220 can be found at http://www.ti.com/product/CC3220.

For IoT development, TI provides the SimpleLink Wi-Fi CC32XX LaunchPad evaluation kit. It's a complete kit for development and debugging. The SimpleLink Wi-Fi CC3200 LaunchPad board is shown in the website `https://www.conrad.de/de/entwicklungsboard-texas-instruments-cc3200-launchxl-1273804.html`.

TI CC3200 is also used by RedBear (`http://redbear.cc`) to develop RedBearLab CC3200 and RedBearLab Wi-Fi Micro boards. These boards have the same functionalities as the SimpleLink Wi-Fi CC3200 LaunchPad board, but exclude the CC3200 debugger tool. The price of these boards is also lower than SimpleLink Wi-Fi CC3200 LaunchPad board's price.

AWS IoT Management Console

AWS IoT Management Console lets you access and manage AWS IoT through a simple and intuitive web-based user interface. This web console can be found at `https://console.aws.amazon.com/iotv2/home`. If you have an active AWS account, you should access a form of AWS IoT Management Console. A screen of AWS IoT Management Console is shown in the following screenshot:

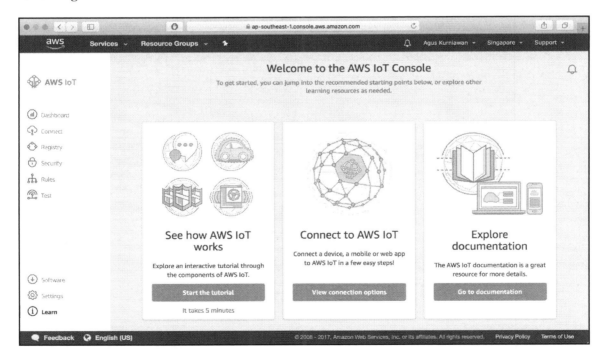

In AWS IoT Management Console, we can manage all IoT devices. This portal provides several features, as follows:

- **Dashboard**: This shows a summary of AWS IoT usage statistics
- **Connect**: This provides information on how to connect to AWS IoT
- **Registry**: This is used to register your new IoT device or to manage existing IoT devices
- **Security**: This configures AWS IoT and IoT devices
- **Rules**: This manages all rules for AWS IoT
- **Test**: This provides a test tool to evaluate your AWS IoT platform

You can see these menus in the following screenshot:

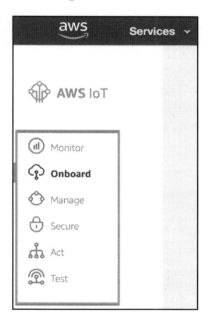

You will probably get different menus on the dashboard. You can change your AWS region in order to get full menus by clicking the menu on the top-right of the dashboard.

We will work with AWS IoT Management Console to manage our IoT projects in the next section.

AWS IoT Device SDK

The AWS server has several components and features. To minimize complexity in development, AWS provides AWS IoT Device SDK for various IoT device platforms. You can use them directly for your IoT platform. There are a lot of objects/classes that you can apply in your IoT program to access AWS IoT. You can find out more about AWS IoT SDK at https://aws.amazon.com/iot/sdk/.

Currently, AWS IoT Device SDK supports the following SDK:

- Embedded C
- Arduino Yún
- Java
- JavaScript
- Python
- iOS
- Android

To work with AWS IoT Device SDK, you should verify whether your IoT device supports this SDK or not. We will focus on applying AWS IoT Device SDK in Chapter 2, *Connecting IoT Devices to AWS IoT Platform*.

Setting up AWS IoT for your IoT project

In this section, you will learn how to set up your IoT project, utilizing the AWS IoT platform. The following is a list of steps to build your AWS IoT project:

1. Register on AWS
2. Select the IoT device
3. Register AWS IoT
4. Create a security certificate
5. Configure security access

Let's go through these steps.

Creating an AWS account

AWS provides a complete solution to build your enterprise system, starting from a virtual machine and enterprise application, to machine learning and IoT. At the time of writing, Amazon offers a free one year trial access called **AWS Free Tier** for a newly registered user. You can access the full features with the limited scheme. You can register a new AWS account and get a free one year trial access at `https://aws.amazon.com`.

Most AWS can be accessed with the AWS Free Tier scheme. I recommend you do so. The AWS Free Tier registration page is shown in the following screenshot:

Selecting an IoT device

The next step is to select your IoT device. Each IoT device has unique capabilities. I suggest that you use the IoT device platform that is recommended by Amazon to minimize problems while developing and deploying. You can use one of the listed devices from `https://aws.amazon.com/iot-platform/getting-started/#kits`. Based on my experience, the Raspberry Pi board or IoT board with the Linux platform is easier, because most AWS IoT Device SDKs are supported.

I will show how various IoT device platforms access AWS IoT, with specific scenarios in this book. Register an IoT device for AWS IoT after you have decided what IoT device model is to be implemented. You should register it in order to obtain access rights in AWS IoT. You can register your IoT device on AWS IoT Management Console with the following steps:

1. Navigate to `https://console.aws.amazon.com/iot`. You should see a form as shown in the following screenshot:

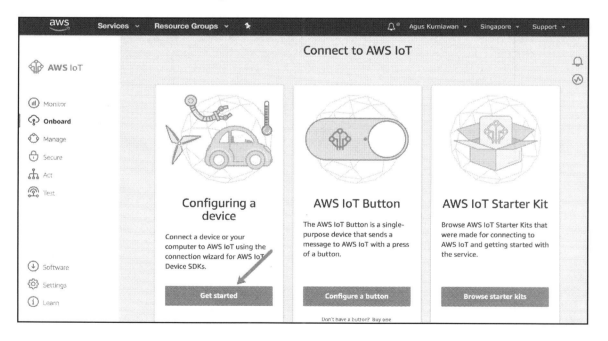

2. Select the **Onboard** option from the left-hand menu. You can click on the **Get started** button within the **Configuring a device** section, which is shown by an arrow in the preceding screenshot.

Then, you will get information about connecting IoT device to AWS IoT, as shown   in the following screenshot:

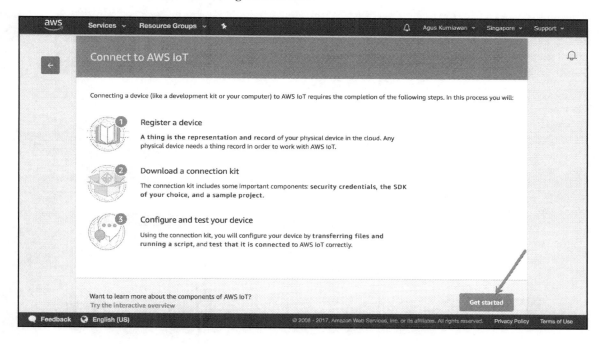

3. Select the development platform of the IoT device and AWS IoT SDK. In this scenario, I use **Linux/OSX** with **Node.js** for AWS IoT SDK:

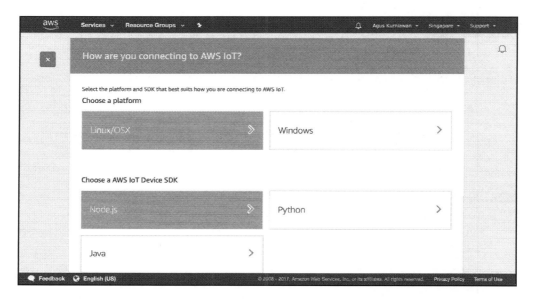

4. Now we create our IoT device name. You should define the IoT device type. To do so, you click on the **Create a type** button:

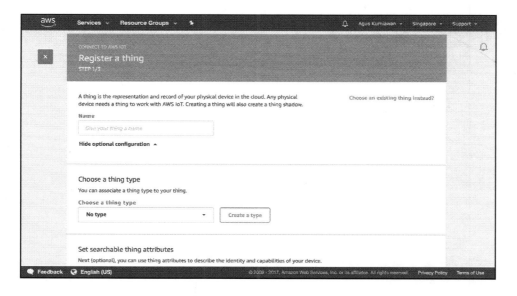

5. Fill out the IoT device type and its description. You may define IoT device attributes. For a demo, we define the following two attributes as shown in the following screenshot:
   - name
   - device-value

If done, save this IoT device type.

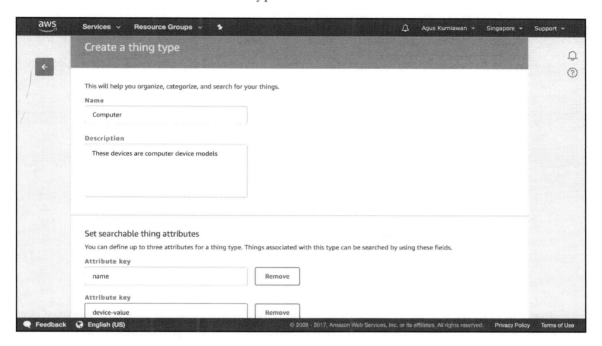

6. Then, go back to your IoT device registering. Fill out the IoT device name and its type. I filled `macos-computer` in the **Name** field, as shown in the following screenshot:

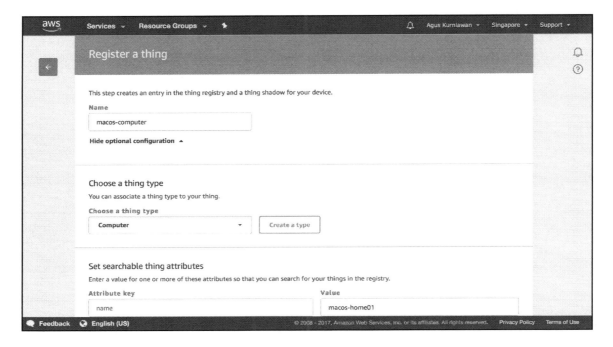

7. If done, you should see your IoT device on the **Manage** | **Things** menu:

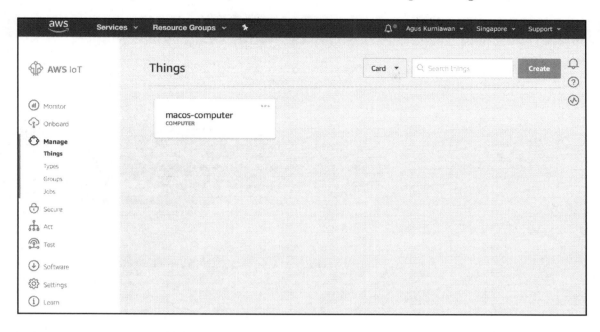

You can add additional IoT devices to simulate the AWS IoT scenario.

Creating a security certificate

Before we use AWS IoT, we should create a security certificate. Then, this certificate will be attached to our registered IoT device. Follow these steps:

1. On AWS IoT Management Console, open your IoT device. Click on the **Security** option on the left-hand menu. You should see a form, as shown in the following screenshot:

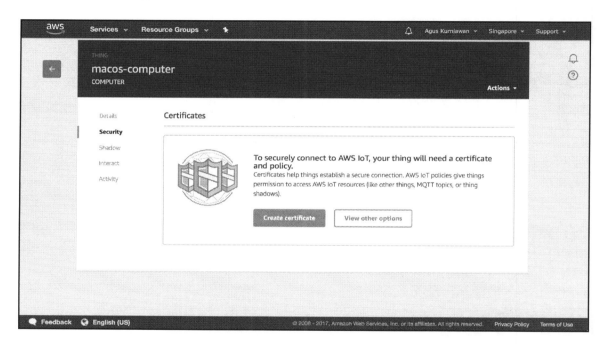

2. You should see a **Create certificate** button. Click on this button. Then, AWS IoT will generate private and public keys for your IoT device. Please download all certificate and key files:

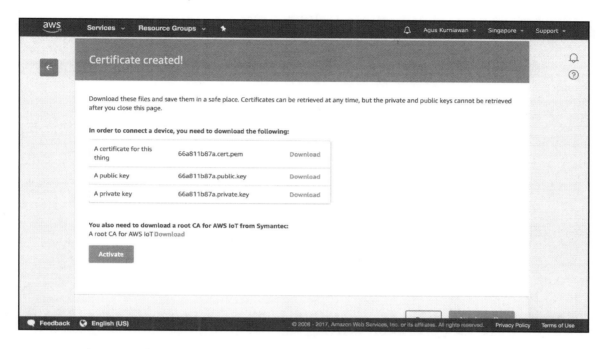

These certificate and key files will be used in our program to access the AWS IoT server. You should get four files, as follows:

- Certificate file (*.pem)
- Certificate public key file (*.key)
- Certificate private key file (*.key)
- Root certificate (*.pem) or (*.crt)

3. Put all these files into a folder. Our program will access these files:

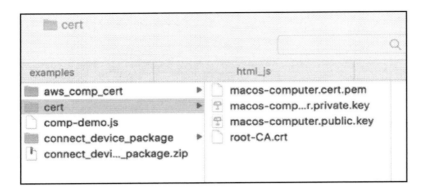

The next step is to write a program. We will do so in the next section.

Configuring security access for AWS IoT

Since AWS IoT applies security to protect its system, we should also comply to configure our AWS IoT security. Some steps are taken to configure our AWS IoT security. We will perform the following tasks:

1. Create a policy
2. Attach a policy to the IoT device certificate
3. Attach the IoT thing to the certificate

To create a policy on AWS IoT, perform the following steps:

1. Click the **Policies** sub-menu from the **Secure** menu, as shown in the following screenshot:

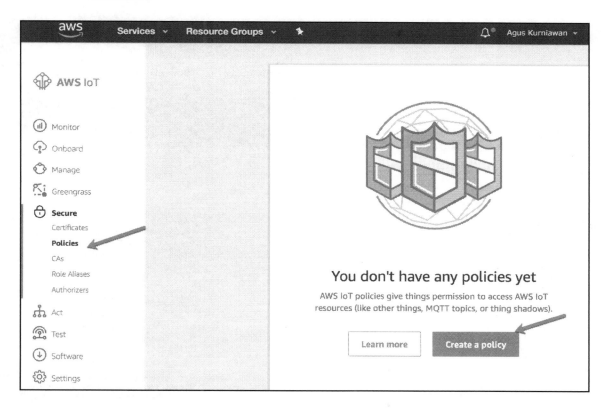

2. Then, you should see a **Create a policy** button. Click on this button.
3. Fill in your policy name. You should add three policy statements, as follows:

   - **iot:Connect**
   - **iot:Subscribe**
   - **iot:Publish**

4. Don't forget to check the **Allow** checkbox for all the preceding policy statements:

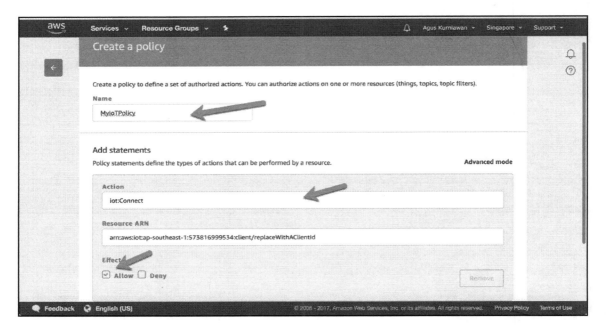

5. When done, save your AWS IoT policy. You should see your created policy on the **Policies** form, as shown in the following screenshot:

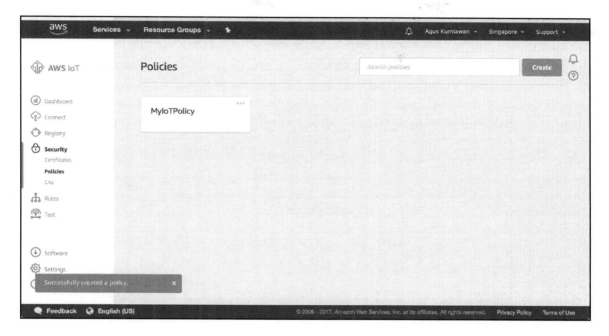

6. The next step is to add our created policy into the IoT device certificate. You can open **Secure | Certificates** on AWS IoT Management Console. Click on the ellipsis (**...**) link so you get a context menu that is shown in the following screenshot. Click on the **Attach policy** option:

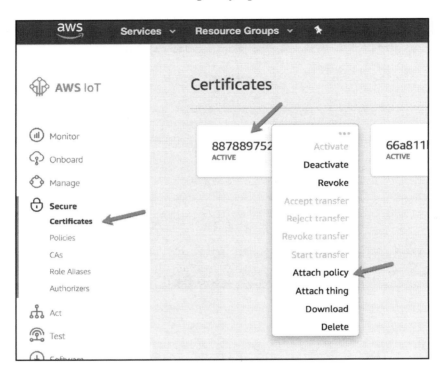

7. Then, you get a dialog box. Select your created policy. When done, click on the **Attach** button to execute this task:

8. The last step is to add our IoT device into a security certificate. Click on the ellipsis (**...**) on your certificate so you get a context menu. Select the **Attach thing** option on context menu:

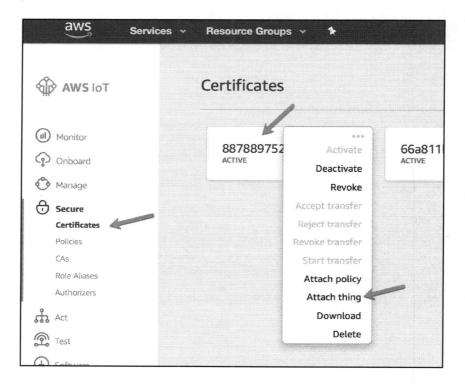

9. Select your IoT device and then click on the **Attach** button to perform this task:

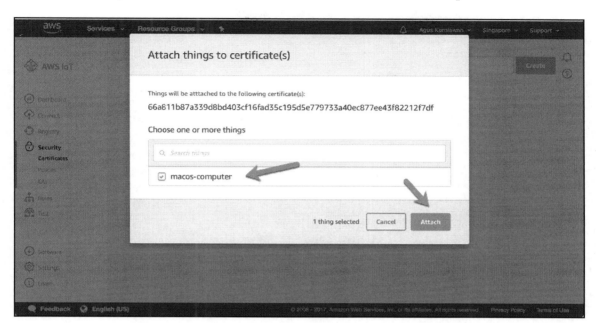

Now your IoT device has a certificate and policy. You can access AWS IoT through the IoT device.

Setting up the development environment

After we have registered all the IoT devices for AWS IoT, we can set up our development environment. Depending on your kind of IoT device, you can install AWS IoT SDK for your device. You can review the details at https://aws.amazon.com/iot/sdk/.

For testing, we use a computer that acts as an IoT thing. The computer will access AWS IoT. To simplify our case, I use JavaScript SDK for AWS IoT, available at https://github.com/aws/aws-iot-device-sdk-js. Since JavaScript SDK for AWS IoT needs Node.js to run the program, your computer should install Node.js runtime. You can download and install Node.js for your platform from https://nodejs.org/.

To install AWS IoT SDK for JavaScript, do so through the npm package. You should install Node.js runtime for your platform. You can type the following command to install AWS IoT SDK for JavaScript:

```
$ npm install aws-iot-device-sdk
```

You can probably run this command at an administrator level if you get an error message due to a security issue.

For the development tool, you can use any text editor to write JavaScript scripts. For instance, you can use Visual Studio Code at https://code.visualstudio.com. You can see my sample JavaScript scripts on Visual Studio Code IDE in the following screenshot:

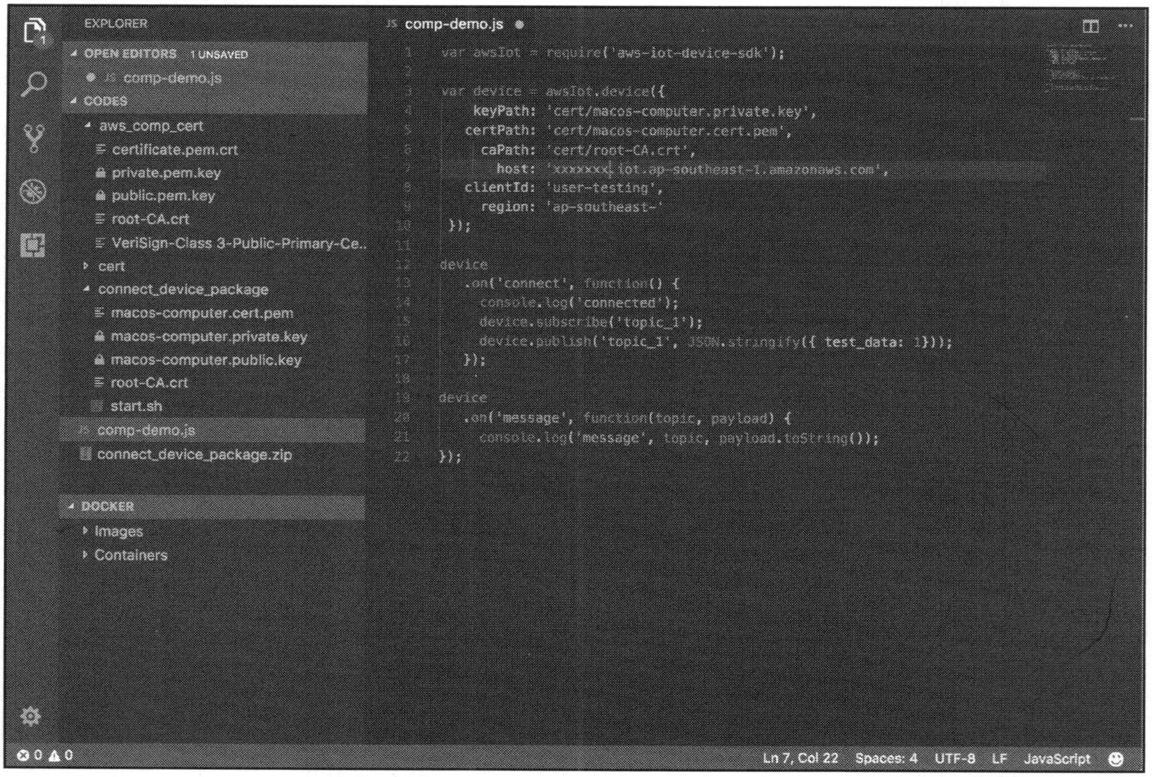

Building an AWS IoT program

After we have configured our AWS IoT and added the IoT device, we can develop a program to access AWS IoT. In this scenario, our computer is used as an IoT thing. We also used Node.js to access AWS IoT, so we need to install AWS IoT SDK for JavaScript. For testing, we will build a Node.js application to access AWS IoT for such purposes as connecting, sending, and receiving.

Now, create a file called `comp-demo.js`. Then, write the following Node.js scripts:

```
var awsIot = require('aws-iot-device-sdk');
var device = awsIot.device({
    keyPath: 'cert/macos-computer.private.key',
   certPath: 'cert/macos-computer.cert.pem',
     caPath: 'cert/root-CA.crt',
       host: 'xxxxxxx.iot.ap-southeast-1.amazonaws.com',
   clientId: 'user-testing',
     region: 'ap-southeast-'
 });
device
   .on('connect', function() {
     console.log('connected');
     device.subscribe('topic_1');
     device.publish('topic_1', JSON.stringify({ test_data: 1}));
   });
device
   .on('message', function(topic, payload) {
     console.log('message', topic, payload.toString());
});
```

Please change the path and certificate files from your AWS IoT on parameters such as `keyPath`, `certPath`, `caPath`, `host`, and `region`. Save this file.

How to work with the program?

Now we will review our program, `comp-demo.js`. The following is a list of steps for the program:

1. Firstly, we apply the required library from AWS IoT SDK for JavaScript. Then, we declare our device based on our IoT thing from AWS IoT:

```
var awsIot = require('aws-iot-device-sdk');
var device = awsIot.device({
    keyPath: 'cert/macos-computer.private.key',
```

```
    certPath: 'cert/macos-computer.cert.pem',
      caPath: 'cert/root-CA.crt',
        host: 'xxxxxxx.iot.ap-southeast-1.amazonaws.com',
    clientId: 'user-testing',
      region: 'ap-southeast-'
});
```

2. We try to connect to AWS IoT. After we are connected, we subscribe a specific topic, for instance, `topic_1`. Then, we send a message by calling the `publish()` function:

```
device
    .on('connect', function() {
      console.log('connected');
      device.subscribe('topic_1');
      device.publish('topic_1', JSON.stringify({ test_data:
1})));
    });
```

3. To receive an incoming message from AWS IoT, we listen to the message event as follows:

```
device
    .on('message', function(topic, payload) {
      console.log('message', topic, payload.toString());
});
```

Testing all

After we write a program, `comp-demo.js`, we can execute this program. Now you can run the program. Type this command:

```
$ node comp-demo.js
```

Make sure all certificate files are on the same path with `comp-demo.js`. If successful, you should see the connected state and receive the incoming message:

```
codes — node comp-demo.js — 80×16
agusk$ node comp-demo.js
connected
message topic_1 {"test_data":1}
```

You can also verify on AWS IoT Management Console about this transaction:

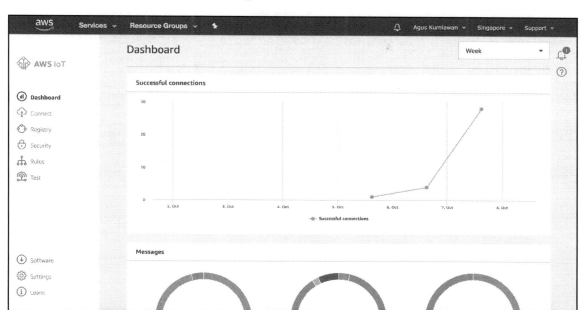

Summary

We have learned what AWS IoT is and explored several IoT device platforms. AWS IoT Management Console and Device SDK were introduced to obtain the essentials of AWS IoT platform.

In the last section, we registered and configured an IoT device. Then, we created a program to access AWS IoT from the IoT device. In the next chapter, we will learn how to connect to AWS IoT from various IoT devices and make interactions.

2
Connecting IoT Devices to AWS IoT Platform

There are many IoT devices on the market. In this chapter, we will learn how to connect several common IoT devices from the market to AWS IoT. Some tricks and demos are provided to show how to work with these IoT devices. Finally, we will build an IoT application by utilizing IoT devices and AWS IoT.

The following is a list of topics that we will explore in this chapter:

- Introducing a connectivity model for AWS IoT
- Selecting your IoT devices for AWS IoT
- Developing AWS IoT for Raspberry Pi 3
- Developing AWS IoT for Arduino
- Developing AWS IoT for ESP32
- Building an IoT project with AWS IoT

Introducing a connectivity model for AWS IoT

AWS IoT provides several connectivity models to enable IoT devices to establish their connection. Currently, AWS IoT offers the following protocols:

- **Message Queuing Telemetry Transport (MQTT)**
- **Hypertext Transfer Protocol (HTTP)**
- MQTT over Websocket

We can build a connectivity model between IoT devices and the AWS IoT backend. We can categorize the IoT device platform into the following three models based on their supported connectivity:

- For an IoT device with network capabilities, if this device has all the support required by AWS IoT, then this device can access AWS IoT directly.
- The second connectivity model is to build a connection to AWS IoT through a gateway. This approach is applied for an IoT device that has network capabilities which are not supported for AWS IoT protocols.
- The last approach is to be applied to IoT devices that do not have network capabilities. We should attach these devices to a network device, such as Raspberry Pi, BeagleBone, and a computer that works as a bridge between the device and AWS IoT.

Selecting your IoT devices for AWS IoT

We already know that there are a lot of IoT devices on the market. To work with AWS IoT, Amazon provides guidelines about a list of IoT devices with supported AWS IoT. You can read it at `https://aws.amazon.com/iot-platform/getting-started/#kits`. Otherwise, you can use own IoT devices and ensure that they are compatible with AWS IoT SDK by referring to `https://aws.amazon.com/iot-platform/sdk/`.

From this, you can make a self-assessment when you select an IoT device for the AWS IoT platform. You can verify your selection with the following questions:

- *Does the IoT device have a network capability?* A network capability probably can identity network features such as Ethernet, Wi-Fi, Bluetooth, Zigbee and LoRa.
- *Does the IoT device network module give support for the AWS IoT protocol?* Make sure your IoT device can communicate with external devices through HTTP, MQTT, or MQTT over Websocket.

If your IoT device does not fit these criteria, your IoT device can connect to AWS IoT using a third approach—attaching your IoT device to a network device, for instance, a computer, and then connecting from a program inside the computer to AWS IoT.

We will explore and review some IoT devices to connect AWS IoT in the next section. The following are the three IoT devices that we will review in this chapter:

- Raspberry Pi 3
- Arduino Yún
- ESP32 board

Configuring IoT devices to AWS IoT

In this section, we will configure an IoT device in order to access AWS IoT. Several steps should be taken to complete the registration process:

1. Firstly, we create a thing type. You can perform this task on the **Manage** | **Types** menu from AWS IoT Console and then click on the **Create** button. Fill in the type name and attributes for your IoT device. For instance, we give a thing type as IoT-Device with name as the thing attribute :

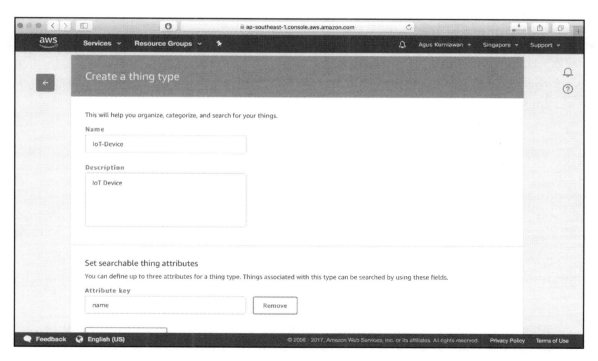

2. After this has been created, you should see it on the **Types** screen from the AWS IoT dashboard, as shown in the following screenshot:

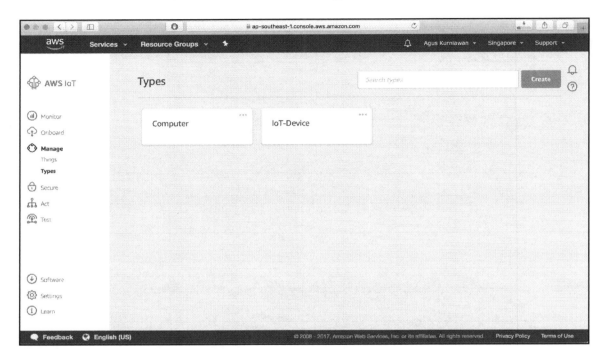

3. Next, we add three IoT devices into AWS IoT. Navigate to **Manage| Things** on the AWS IoT dashboard. Then, you add a thing name and its attribute as shown in the screenshot below the table. The following is our configuration of IoT devices:

Device name	Thing name	Thing attribute
Raspberry Pi 3	raspberry-pi	pi01
Arduino Yún	arduino-yun	arduino01
ESP32 board	esp32	esp32-01

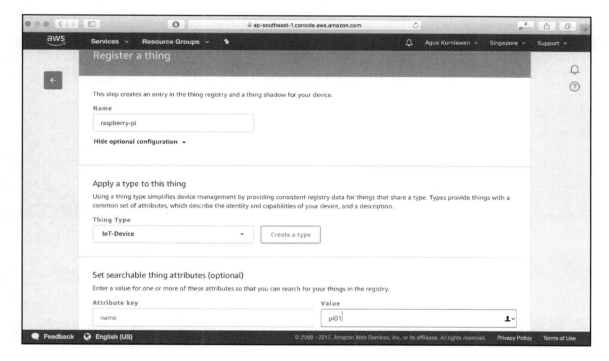

4. After we have added three IoT devices, you should see these devices on the **Things** dashboard from the AWS IoT Management Console, as shown in the following screenshot:

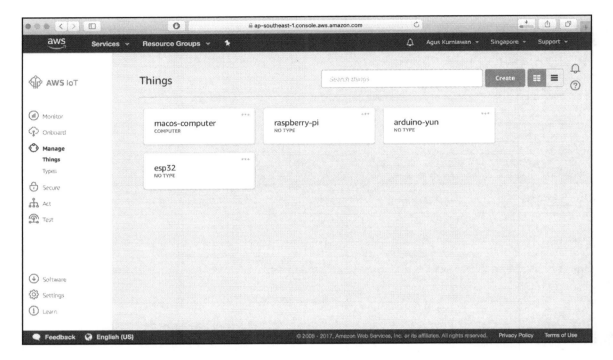

5. The next step is to add our IoT devices to a security certificate. Since we have created a security certificate in `Chapter 1`, *Getting Started with AWS IoT*, we can use that. We add our three devices into our existing certificate by clicking on the certificate, which locates on the **Secure | Certificates** menu from AWS IoT, so you should see a context menu, shown in the following screenshot:

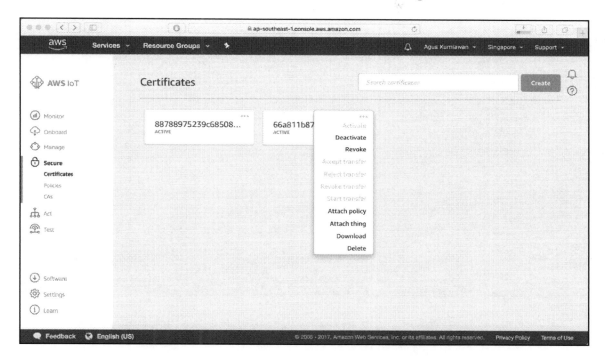

6. Select the **Attach thing** menu on the context menu. Then, check all the devices. Click on the **Attach** button once done, as shown in the following screenshot:

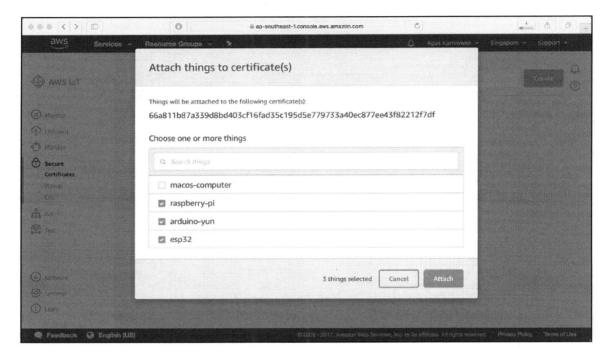

7. We can verify whether our devices are already added or not. You can check it on the **Things** screen from your certificate on AWS IoT Management Console, as shown in the following screenshot:

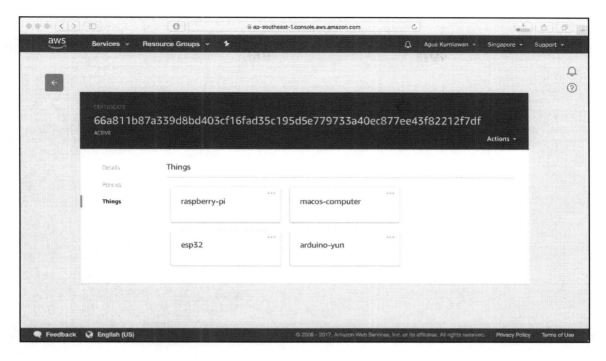

Now our devices are ready for AWS IoT development.

AWS IoT development for Raspberry Pi 3

Raspberry Pi is a famous IoT development. At a low price, you can obtain a minicomputer. Some demo scenarios in this book can be implemented using a desktop computer. Currently, Raspberry Pi 3 is the latest product from Raspberry Pi Foundation. For further information about Raspberry Pi and getting this board, I recommend that you visit the official website at `http://raspberrypi.org`.

Raspberry Pi 3 can be deployed on various OSes, such as Linux and Windows 10 IoT Core. In this chapter, we will focus on Raspberry Pi 3 with Linux as the OS. We use Raspbian Linux. You can download and install it at `https://www.raspberrypi.org/downloads/raspbian/`.

Raspbian Linux can work as a console or in desktop mode. You can see Raspbian Linux on Raspberry Pi 3 in the following screenshot:

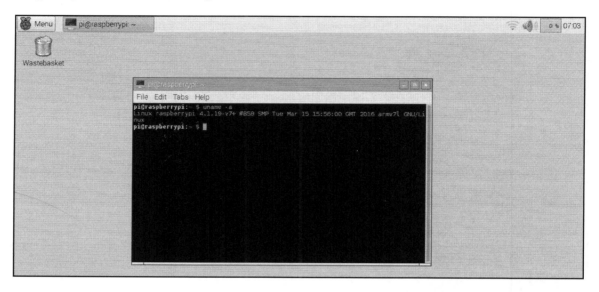

The corresponding AWS IoT SDK is available at `https://aws.amazon.com/iot-platform/sdk/`. There are SDKs for Raspberry Pi 3 with the following approaches:

- **AWS IoT SDK JavaScript**: This is used if you want to develop a program-based JavaScript, such as Node.js
- **AWS IoT SDK Python**: If you want to develop Python for AWS IoT, you can use this SDK on your Raspberry Pi 3
- **AWS IoT SDK Java**: For Java developers, this SDK can extend your skill to develop Java applications to connect to AWS IoT
- **AWS IoT SDK Embedded C**: If you are familiar with C programming, you can choose this SDK to develop an AWS IoT program

Each AWS IoT SDK has a different approach to deploy it on your device. You can follow the guidelines in the documentation for each AWS IoT SDK.

In this section, we use AWS IoT SDK JavaScript on Raspberry Pi 3. The AWS IoT SDK JavaScript installation process is the same as the installation process on a computer. Make sure your Raspberry Pi has Node.js installed. Since Raspbian Linux on Raspberry Pi has Node.js legacy installed, we should uninstall it and then install the latest Node.js. You can uninstall Node.js legacy by typing the following commands:

```
$ sudo apt-get remove nodered -y
$ sudo apt-get remove nodejs nodejs-legacy -y
$ sudo apt-get remove npm -y
```

To install the latest Node.js on Raspberry Pi, we can use Node.js from the Nodesource distributor, available at https://github.com/nodesource/distributions. Type the following commands:

```
$ sudo su -
$ curl -sL https://deb.nodesource.com/setup_8.x | sudo bash -
$ apt-get install nodejs -y
$ node -v
$ npm -v
$ exit
```

If successful, you should see the latest Node.js and **Node Package Manager** (**NPM**), as shown in the following screenshot:

```
root@raspberrypi:~# apt-get install nodejs -y
Reading package lists... Done
Building dependency tree
Reading state information... Done
The following NEW packages will be installed:
  nodejs
0 upgraded, 1 newly installed, 0 to remove and 80 not upgraded.
Need to get 11.2 MB of archives.
After this operation, 53.6 MB of additional disk space will be used.
Get:1 https://deb.nodesource.com/node_8.x/ jessie/main nodejs armhf 8.7.0-1nodes
ource1 [11.2 MB]
Fetched 11.2 MB in 41s (269 kB/s)
Selecting previously unselected package nodejs.
(Reading database ... 178439 files and directories currently installed.)
Preparing to unpack .../nodejs_8.7.0-1nodesource1_armhf.deb ...
Unpacking nodejs (8.7.0-1nodesource1) ...
Processing triggers for man-db (2.7.5-1~bpo8+1) ...
Setting up nodejs (8.7.0-1nodesource1) ...
root@raspberrypi:~# node -v
v8.7.0
root@raspberrypi:~# npm -v
5.4.2
root@raspberrypi:~#
```

After you have the latest Node.js on Raspberry Pi 3, you can install AWS IoT SDK JavaScript through NPM. This SDK can be found at `https://github.com/aws/aws-iot-device-sdk-js`. To install this SDK, type the following command on the Terminal of Raspberry Pi 3:

```
$ npm install aws-iot-device-sdk
```

For testing, we use the same program from `Chapter 1`, *Getting Started with AWS IoT*. You can write this complete program. You should change paths for the certificate, private key, and AWS IoT host. These security certificate files are obtained from AWS IoT. You can read about this in `Chapter 1`, *Getting Started with AWS IoT*.

The following is the complete program for our testing:

```
var awsIot = require('aws-iot-device-sdk');

var device = awsIot.device({
 keyPath: 'cert/private.key',
 certPath: 'cert/cert.pem',
 caPath: 'cert/root-CA.pem',
 host: '<host-aws-iot-server>',
 clientId: 'user-testing',
 region: 'ap-southeast-'
 });

device
 .on('connect', function() {
 console.log('connected');
 device.subscribe('topic_1');
 device.publish('topic_1', JSON.stringify({ test_data: 1}));
 });

device
 .on('message', function(topic, payload) {
 console.log('message', topic, payload.toString());
 });
```

Save this program as the `pi-demo.js` file.

The screenshot of the preceding code is shown as follows:

```
GNU nano 2.2.6                 File: pi-demo.js

var awsIot = require('aws-iot-device-sdk');

var device = awsIot.device({
    keyPath: 'cert/macos-computer.private.key',
   certPath: 'cert/macos-computer.cert.pem',
     caPath: 'cert/root-CA.pem',
       host: '            iot.ap-southeast-1.amazonaws.com',
   clientId: 'user-testing',
     region: 'ap-southeast-'
 });

device
   .on('connect', function() {
     console.log('connected');
     device.subscribe('topic_1');
     device.publish('topic_1', JSON.stringify({ test_data: 1}));
   });

device
                        [ Read 22 lines ]
^G Get Help   ^O WriteOut   ^R Read File  ^Y Prev Page  ^K Cut Text   ^C Cur Pos
^X Exit       ^J Justify    ^W Where Is   ^V Next Page  ^U UnCut Text ^T To Spell
```

Now you can run this program by typing the following command:

```
$ node pi-demo.js
```

If we succeed, the program will present a message, as shown in the following screenshot:

```
pi@raspberrypi:~/Documents/awsiot $ node pi-demo.js
connected
message topic_1 {"test_data":1}
```

You also can verify this by opening the **Monitor** dashboard from AWS IoT Management Console. You should see a number of connections to your server:

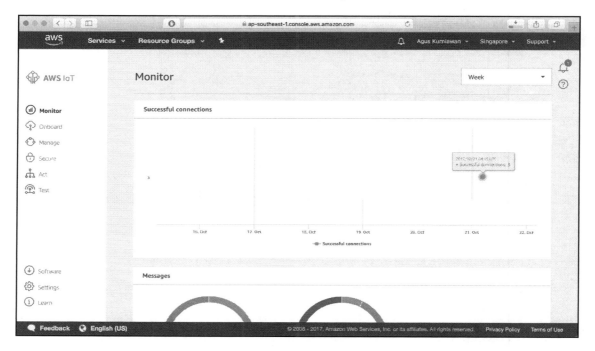

AWS IoT development for Arduino

Most IoT device developments use the Arduino board as the board target. Since Arduino shares schemes and designs, the makers make their own boards with custom Arduino models. Arduino models range from the basic Arduino board model to the advanced Arduino board model. The Arduino board is the best choice to introduce IoT development.

In this section, we will explore how to use Arduino Yún to interact with AWS IoT. For further information about Arduino Yún, I recommend that you read the official documentation at https://www.arduino.cc/en/Guide/ArduinoYun.

To work with AWS IoT using Arduino Yún, we perform the following steps:

1. Install the Arduino software
2. Connect Arduino Yún to a network through Ethernet or a Wi-Fi module
3. Configure Arduino Yún for AWS IoT SDK
4. Build a program for Arduino Yún

Each step will be performed. Now, you can follow the steps in detail, as follows:

1. Firstly, you should install the Arduino software for your OS platform. You can download it at `https://www.arduino.cc/en/Main/Software`.
2. The next step is to connect your Arduino Yún to the existing network. You should join your Arduino Yún into an existing Wi-Fi hotspot. Then, configure your Arduino Yún to join the Wi-Fi network. You can also connect this board to a network through the Ethernet module:

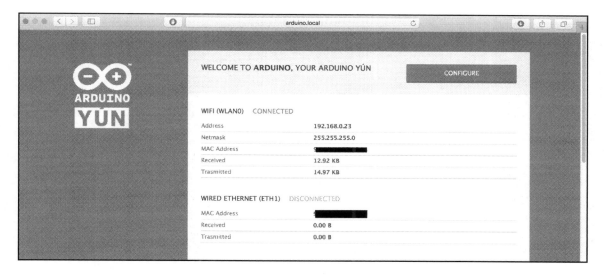

Make sure your computer and Arduino Yún have the same network segment so you can access Arduino Yún over the network.

3. The next step is to configure Arduino Yún for AWS IoT. You should install AWS IoT SDK for Arduino Yún at `https://github.com/aws/aws-iot-device-sdk-arduino-yun`. You can download the latest AWS IoT SDK for Arduino Yún at `https://s3.amazonaws.com/aws-iot-device-sdk-arduino-yun/AWS-IoT-Arduino-Yun-SDK-latest.zip`.

4. Extract a ZIP file into a certain folder. In `Chapter 1`, *Getting Started with AWS IoT*, we have the certificate and private key files for AWS IoT. Put them in the `AWS-IoT-Arduino-Yun-SDK/AWS-IoT-Python-Runtime/certs` folder from the extracted AWS IoT SDK for Arduino Yún .

5. Now, we configure and upload our certificate and private key files into Arduino Yún. For Mac and Linux, you can open the Terminal and navigate to a folder where the SDK file is extracted. You should see the `AWSIoTArduinoYunInstallAll.sh` file. Then, execute this file using the following commands:

```
$ chmod 755 AWSIoTArduinoYunInstallAll.sh
$ ./AWSIoTArduinoYunInstallAll.sh <Board IP> <UserName> <Board
Password>
```

In the preceding code, `<Board IP>` is the IP address of your Arduino Yún. `<UserName>` and `<Board Password>` are the username and password to access your Arduino Yún. By default, if you do not change the password, the username is `root` and the password is `arduino`. This process will take several minutes. Please do not close the process.

6. For Windows, you can use Putty and WinSCP to configure AWS IoT on Arduino Yún . You can download Putty at `http://www.chiark.greenend.org.uk/%7Esgtatham/putty/download.html` and WinSCP at `http://winscp.net/eng/download.php`. Then, you can type the following commands:

```
$ opkg update
$ opkg install distribute
$ opkg install python-openssl
$ easy_install pip
$ pip install AWSIoTPythonSDK==1.0.0
```

The following is a sample of the executing output on macOS:

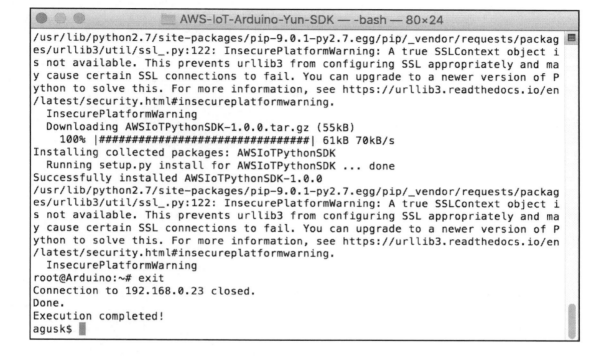

7. For a demo, we use a sample program from AWS IoT SDK for Arduino Yún. It is
   called BasicPubSub. You can find it on the **File| Examples| AWS-IoT-Arduino-
   Yun-Library** menu from the Arduino IDE. You should see the BasicPubSub
   menu. Click on it so you can open the BasicPubSub program, as shown in the
   following screenshot:

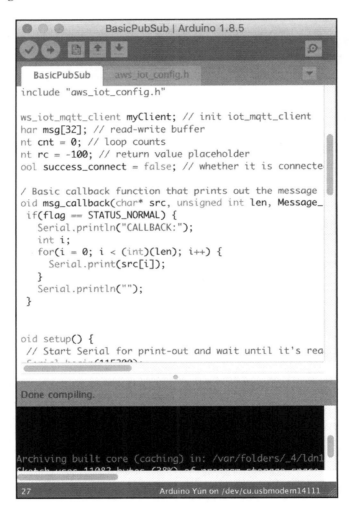

8. You can see that there are two files—BasicPubSub.ino and aws_iot_config.h. The following is a program from the BasicPubSub.ino file:

```
. . .

aws_iot_mqtt_client myClient; // init iot_mqtt_client
char msg[32]; // read-write buffer
int cnt = 0; // loop counts
int rc = -100; // return value placeholder
bool success_connect = false; // whether it is connected

// Basic callback function that prints out the message
void msg_callback(char* src, unsigned int len, Message_status_t
flag) {
 if(flag == STATUS_NORMAL) {
 Serial.println("CALLBACK:");
 int i;
 for(i = 0; i < (int)(len); i++) {
 Serial.print(src[i]);
 }
 Serial.println("");
 }
}


. . .
void loop() {
 if(success_connect) {
 // Generate a new message in each loop and publish to "topic1"
 sprintf(msg, "new message %d", cnt);
 if((rc = myClient.publish("topic1", msg, strlen(msg), 1,
false)) != 0) {
 Serial.println(F("Publish failed!"));
 Serial.println(rc);
 }

. . .

 delay(1000);
```

9. Now we can open the `aws_iot_config.h` file. We should configure the certificate and private key files on the `aws_iot_config.h` file. Change `AWS_IOT_MQTT_HOST` for the IoT endpoint. Also, change the `AWS_IOT_CERTIFICATE_FILENAME` and `AWS_IOT_PRIVATE_KEY_FILENAME` values for the certificate and private key files for your IoT device:

```
#ifndef config_usr_h
#define config_usr_h

// Copy and paste your configuration into this file
//================================================================
==
#define AWS_IOT_MQTT_HOST "<aws-iot-host>" // your endpoint
#define AWS_IOT_MQTT_PORT 8883 // your port
#define AWS_IOT_CLIENT_ID "My_ClientID" // your client ID
#define AWS_IOT_MY_THING_NAME "My_Board" // your thing name
#define AWS_IOT_ROOT_CA_FILENAME "root-CA.crt" // your root-CA
filename
#define AWS_IOT_CERTIFICATE_FILENAME "thing.cert.pem" // your
certificate filename
#define AWS_IOT_PRIVATE_KEY_FILENAME "private.key" // your
private key filename
//================================================================
==
// SDK config, DO NOT modify it
#define AWS_IOT_PATH_PREFIX "../certs/"
#define AWS_IOT_ROOT_CA_PATH AWS_IOT_PATH_PREFIX
AWS_IOT_ROOT_CA_FILENAME // use this in config call
#define AWS_IOT_CERTIFICATE_PATH AWS_IOT_PATH_PREFIX
AWS_IOT_CERTIFICATE_FILENAME // use this in config call
#define AWS_IOT_PRIVATE_KEY_PATH AWS_IOT_PATH_PREFIX
AWS_IOT_PRIVATE_KEY_FILENAME // use this in config call

#endif
```

Save all the changes.

10. To execute the program, compile and upload this sketch program into Arduino Yún. After it is uploaded, you can open the Serial Monitor tool with baud rate 115200. You can see the program output on the Serial Monitor tool:

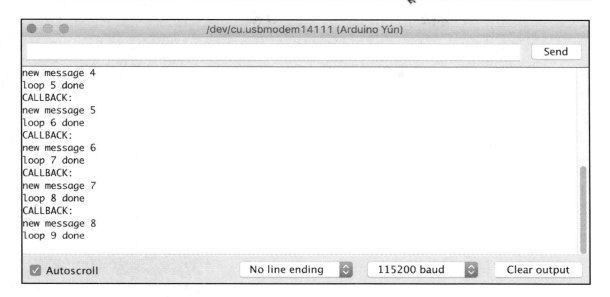

You can verify that this is executing by opening AWS IoT Console to see the incoming messages from Arduino Yún .

AWS IoT development for boards based on ESP32

The ESP32 chip is an MCU with Wi-Fi and Bluetooth network modules. This chip is developed by Espressif. For further information about the ESP32 chip, I recommend that you read the product documentation at http://espressif.com/en/products/hardware/esp32/overview.

There are a lot of boards based on ESP32. You can find various boards based on ESP32 from SparkFun, Adafruit, or embedded companies from China. To work with AWS IoT on the ESP32 chip, we can apply the Mongoose OS platform from Cesanta. You can review the details of this platform on the official website at https://mongoose-os.com.

Cesanta provides an IoT kit-based ESP32 chip, called **Mongoose OS ESP32-DevKitC**. The software of Mongoose OS is built from Node.js/JavaScript. To configure this board connecting to AWS IoT, you can follow the instructions at https://mongoose-os.com/software.html.

Building an IoT project with AWS IoT

In this section, we will try to develop a simple IoT application by applying the AWS IoT platform. We will deploy the IoT program on several IoT devices. These devices will use sensors to sense the physical environment, and then send a result of the sensing to AWS IoT. We will also create a small application to listen to incoming messages from AWS IoT. This is called the **sensor subscriber** application.

You can see a general demo architecture in the following figure. For testing, we use Arduino Yún as the IoT device node:

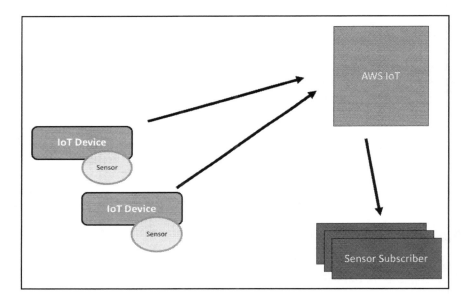

We will build each component in the next section.

Configuring AWS IoT

We should configure your AWS IoT. We already configured this in Chapter 1, *Getting Started with AWS IoT,* and in the first section in this chapter. The idea is to register each IoT device and application to AWS IoT Console. After configuration, we should get the certificate and private key files that will apply in our program.

Developing the Arduino program

For the IoT node device, we apply Arduino Yún with the DHT22 sensor that provides temperature and humidity sensing. You can find DHT22 easily on an online electronic store or at a local store.

The general DHT22 sensor scheme is described in the following image. The third pin is unused. This sensor will be attached to Arduino Yún :

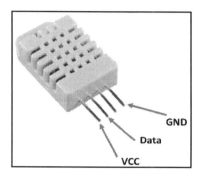

Now we can write the Arduino program. You can proceed with the following steps:

1. To use the DHT sensor with the Arduino board, we use the DHT library from Adafruit. You can find it at `https://github.com/adafruit/DHT-sensor-library`. You can install it by downloading the DHT source from GitHub. You also can install it through the Arduino IDE library. Type `DHT` and select DHT library from Adafruit:

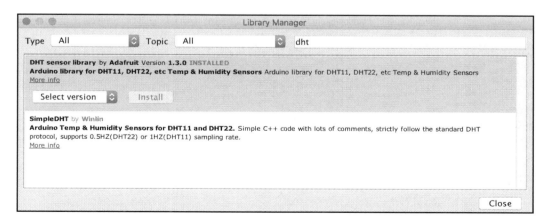

2. To work with the DHT library from Adafruit, you should download the `Adafruit_Sensor.h` file from `https://github.com/adafruit/Adafruit_Sensor`. Copy `Adafruit_Sensor.h` into the `DHT_sensor_library` folder in the Arduino libraries.

3. Now we build the wiring for our demo. Attach DHT22 into a breadboard, and then connect to Arduino through jumper cables. The following is our wiring:
   - DHT22 VCC is connected to Arduino 5V pin
   - DHT22 GND is connected to Arduino GND pin
   - DHT22 Data is connected to Arduino digital pin 10

   You can see the wiring implementation in the following image:

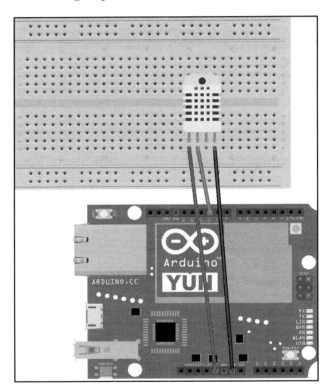

4. The next step is to develop a sketch program. We modify from the previous program, BasicPubSub. We change the topic1 channel to the sensorroom channel. Before we send data to AWS IoT, we read temperature through DHT22:

   1. Firstly, we add the DHT library and initialize our library:

```
#include "DHT.h"
#define DHTTYPE DHT22
#define DHTPIN 10
DHT dht(DHTPIN, DHTTYPE);

void setup() {
 ....
 dht.begin();

....
 if((rc = myClient.subscribe("sensorroom", 1,
msg_callback)) != 0) {
 Serial.println("Subscribe failed!");
 Serial.println(rc);
 }
}
```

   2. On the loop() function, we read the temperature and then send it to AWS IoT:

```
void loop() {
 if(success_connect) {

 char floatBuffer[8];
 float t = dht.readTemperature();
 byte precision = 2;
 dtostrf(t, precision+3, precision, floatBuffer);

 Serial.print("Temperature: ");
 Serial.println(t);
 if (isnan(t)) {
 Serial.println("Failed to read from DHT sensor!");
 return;
 }

 sprintf(msg, "Temp: %s", floatBuffer);
 if((rc = myClient.publish("sensorroom", msg,
strlen(msg), 1, false)) != 0) {
 Serial.println(F("Publish failed!"));
 Serial.println(rc);
 }
```

```
   . . .
   }
  }
```

3. The following is the code snippet for the Arduino sketch:

```
...
aws_iot_mqtt_client myClient; // init iot_mqtt_client
char msg[32]; // read-write buffer
int cnt = 0; // loop counts
int rc = -100; // return value placeholder
bool success_connect = false; // whether it is
connected

#define DHTTYPE DHT22
#define DHTPIN 10
DHT dht(DHTPIN, DHTTYPE);
...

  // Get a chance to run a callback
  if((rc = myClient.yield()) != 0) {
  Serial.println("Yield failed!");
  Serial.println(rc);
  }
  Serial.print("Sent: ");
  Serial.println(msg);

  delay(3000);
  }
 }
```

Now you can open the `aws_iot_config.h` file. You should configure the certificate and private key files, including your AWS IoT endpoint on AWS_IOT_MQTT_HOST.

Save this program as `IoTNode`.

Developing a sensor subscriber

To see what sensor data is sent by Arduino Yún , we can create a simple program to subscribe a message on a specific channel. We already define the sensorroom channel as the sensor channel. Using the previous program from Chapter 1, *Getting Started with AWS IoT,* we can develop a program to subscribe the sensorroom channel and then listen to the incoming messages from AWS IoT. We use the Node.js application to communicate with AWS IoT.

Write the following scripts for the complete program:

```
var awsIot = require('aws-iot-device-sdk');

var device = awsIot.device({
 keyPath: 'cert/private.key',
 certPath: 'cert/cert.pem',
 caPath: 'cert/root-CA.pem',
 host: '<host-aws-iot-server>',
 clientId: 'user-testing',
 region: 'ap-southeast-'
 });

device
 .on('connect', function() {
 console.log('connected');
 device.subscribe('sensorroom');
 });

device
 .on('message', function(topic, payload) {
 console.log('recv:', topic, payload.toString());
});

console.log('Sensor subscriber started.');
```

Save this program as the sensor-subscriber.js file.

Testing

After we deploy the sketch program into Arduino Yún , you can run the sensor subscriber application first. Type the following command on your Terminal or Command Prompt for Windows:

```
$ node sensor-subscriber.js
```

The sketch program will sense `Temperature` and send it to AWS IoT. You can see it on the Serial Monitor Tool. The following screenshot shows `Temperature` from the result of the measurement:

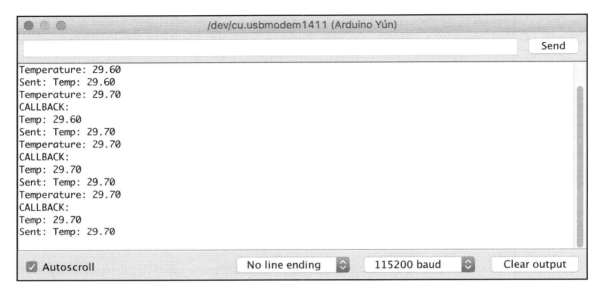

A sensor subscriber application will get sensor data from AWS IoT since it has already subscribed to `sensorroom`. You can see it in the following screenshot:

Summary

We have reviewed some IoT devices and shown how to send data to AWS IoT. Each IoT device has its own AWS SDK to ensure communication with AWS IoT. Finally, we built a simple IoT application to send the sensor data, temperature, to AWS IoT. To read the sensor data, we have a Node.js application to subscribe the sensor channel in order to access the sensor data from AWS IoT.

In the next chapter, we will learn how to build AWS Greengrass and interact with IoT devices.

3
Optimizing IoT Computing Using AWS Greengrass

Some companies probably have security policies that do not allow some internal devices, such as computers and IoT devices, to connect to the internet directly. To solve these issues, they provide proxy or bridge servers to accommodate connectivity between internet devices and internet networks. For IoT cases, we can build a gateway server to serve those requests. In this chapter, we will learn how IoT devices connect to AWS and perform computation locally. We will explore and implement AWS Greengrass to serve all IoT devices to perform AWS computations. We will deploy AWS Greengrass and use Raspberry Pi 3 as AWS Greengrass Core.

The following is a list of topics that we will cover in this chapter:

- Introducing AWS Greengrass
- Exploring supported IoT devices for AWS Greengrass
- Deploying AWS Greengrass on Raspberry Pi 3
- Accessing AWS Greengrass
- Building IoT projects with AWS Greengrass

Introducing AWS Greengrass

AWS Greengrass is one of the AWS services that enables you to build the AWS IoT server locally. This solution has an advantage, because our IoT devices should not connect to AWS IoT directly.

AWS Greengrass acts as a bridge or gateway for connected IoT devices. It offers AWS computation, such as AWS Lambda. We can deploy our own service over AWS Lambda on AWS Greengrass. AWS Greengrass can be implemented on a computer or device-based ARM CPU. All devices that are used for AWS Greengrass should be registered to AWS IoT. IoT devices have access to AWS Greengrass and AWS Greengrass needs to be configured in one group so that both the IoT devices and AWS Greengrass can communicate with each other.

A general overview of AWS Greengrass is depicted in the following figure. Each IoT device can connect to AWS Greengrass to perform computation without connecting to the AWS server. IoT devices and AWS Greengrass can only communicate within the Greengrass Group:

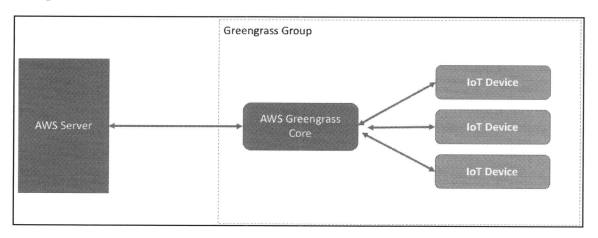

AWS Greengrass Console can be accessed at `https://console.aws.amazon.com/greengrass`. You can review and explore this console. We can manage all AWS Greengrass and IoT devices. The AWS Greengrass console can be seen in the following screenshot:

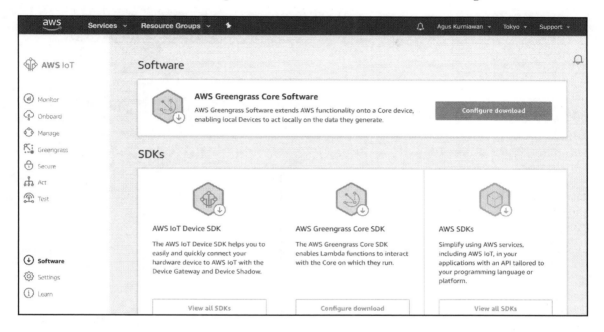

Not all AWS IoT regions are supported for AWS Greengrass. You can check this while you deploy AWS Greengrass on AWS IoT Management Console. You can change the AWS location on the top menu, as shown in the following screenshot:

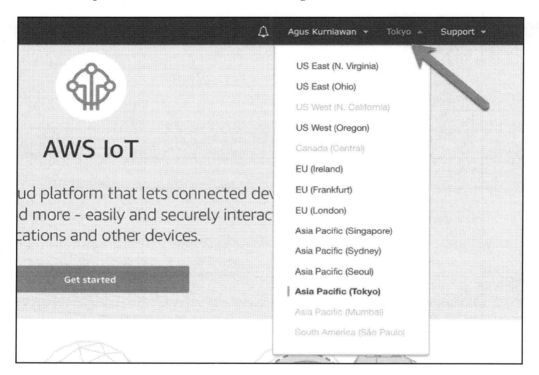

Exploring supported IoT devices for AWS Greengrass

To run AWS Greengrass on a machine, we should install AWS Greengrass Core. This software can run on x86_64, ARMv7, and AArch64 (ARMv8) architecture platforms. It also supports Ubuntu 14.04 LTS, Jessie Kernel 4.1/4.4, and other Linux distributions based on Kernel 4.4 or later versions.

The list of supported IoT boards for AWS Greengrass can be found at `https://aws.amazon.com/greengrass/faqs/`. This book will use Raspberry Pi 3 for targeting AWS Greengrass.

Deploying AWS Greengrass on Raspberry Pi 3

In this section, we will deploy AWS Greengrass on Raspberry Pi 3 Model B. To implement AWS Greengrass deployment, we have the Raspberry Pi 3 board and an active AWS account. There are several steps to deploy AWS Greengrass on Raspberry Pi 3. Perform the following steps:

1. Prepare Raspberry Pi 3
2. Configure Raspberry Pi 3 and other IoT devices to AWS IoT
3. Install AWS Greengrass

These steps will be explained in the following sections.

Preparing Raspberry Pi 3

The Raspberry Pi 3 board can run on several OSes. A list of supported OSes for Raspberry Pi 3 can be found at `https://www.raspberrypi.org/downloads/`. To work with AWS Greengrass Core, it is recommended that you install the latest Raspbian Linux OS for Raspberry Pi, which can be found at `https://www.raspberrypi.org/downloads/raspbian/`. For a refresher on installation on Raspberry Pi 3, I recommend you follow the instructions mentioned at `https://www.raspberrypi.org/documentation/installation/installing-images/README.md`.

Now we will prepare to deploy AWS Greengrass Core on Raspberry Pi 3. Follow these steps:

1. You should have installed Raspbian on Raspberry Pi 3. If you have not, you can install it by following the guidelines at `https://www.raspberrypi.org/documentation/installation/installing-images/README.md`. If you have installed Raspbian on Raspberry Pi 3, make sure that the OS has Linux kernel 4.4.11+ or later with OverlayFS and the user namespace enabled. You can verify this using the following command on the Terminal:

   ```
   $ uname -a
   ```

You should see the kernel version on the Terminal. For instance, you can see my kernel version, which is 4.9.41, from the Raspbian OS in the following screenshot:

```
● ● ●        agusk — pi@raspberrypi: ~ — ssh pi@192.168.0.21 — 80×19
[pi@raspberrypi:~ $ uname -a
Linux raspberrypi 4.9.41-v7+ #1023 SMP Tue Aug 8 16:00:15 BST 2017 armv7l GNU/Li
nux
pi@raspberrypi:~ $
```

2. You also can upgrade Raspbian Linux in order to work with AWS Greengrass. You can type the commands as follows:

```
$ sudo apt-get update
$ sudo apt-get upgrade
$ sudo BRANCH=next rpi-update
```

This operation needs internet access, so your Raspberry Pi should be connected to the internet.

3. The next step is to create a user named ggc_user and a group named ggc_group. Type the following commands on the Raspberry Pi Terminal:

```
$ sudo adduser --system ggc_user
$ sudo addgroup --system ggc_group
```

You can see the executed commands in the following screenshot:

```
● ● ●        agusk — pi@raspberrypi: ~ — ssh pi@192.168.0.73 — 80×19
pi@raspberrypi:~ $ sudo adduser --system ggc_user
Adding system user `ggc_user' (UID 111) ...
Adding new user `ggc_user' (UID 111) with group `nogroup' ...
Creating home directory `/home/ggc_user' ...
pi@raspberrypi:~ $ sudo addgroup --system ggc_group
Adding group `ggc_group' (GID 116) ...
Done.
pi@raspberrypi:~ $
```

4. AWS Greengrass requires local storage to perform local processing. You can install SQLite on Raspberry Pi. For this, type the following command:

```
$ sudo apt-get install sqlite3
```

5. Since AWS Greengrass requires a high-security environment, Raspberry Pi should be configured to activate hardlink/softlink protection. You can perform it by opening the /etc/sysctl.d/98-rpi.conf file:

```
$ sudo nano /etc/sysctl.d/98-rpi.conf
```

6. Then, add these scripts on that file:

```
fs.protected_hardlinks = 1
fs.protected_symlinks = 1
```

You can see this in the following screenshot:

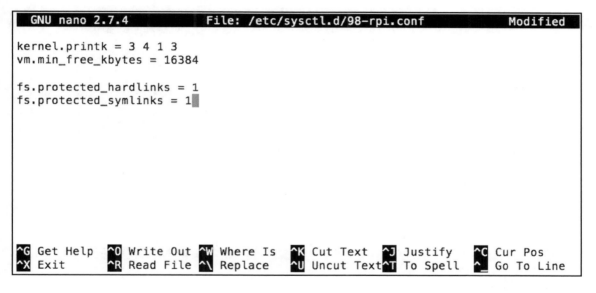

7. Save, and reboot your Raspberry Pi:

```
$ sudo reboot
```

8. After reboot, please type the following command:

```
$ sudo sysctl -a | grep fs
```

You should see our added parameters in the Terminal, as in the following screenshot:

```
fs.nfs.nlm_udpport = 0
fs.nfs.nsm_local_state = 0
fs.nfs.nsm_use_hostnames = 0
fs.nr_open = 1048576
fs.overflowgid = 65534
fs.overflowuid = 65534
fs.pipe-max-size = 1048576
fs.pipe-user-pages-hard = 0
fs.pipe-user-pages-soft = 16384
fs.protected_hardlinks = 1
fs.protected_symlinks = 1
fs.quota.allocated_dquots = 0
fs.quota.cache_hits = 0
fs.quota.drops = 0
fs.quota.free_dquots = 0
fs.quota.lookups = 0
fs.quota.reads = 0
fs.quota.syncs = 0
fs.quota.warnings = 1
```

The next step is to configure and register Raspberry Pi to AWS IoT in order to enable AWS Greengrass. We will perform this task in the next section.

Configuring Raspberry Pi 3 and IoT devices to AWS IoT

All devices that are used for AWS Greengrass should be registered to AWS IoT. A result of the registration will be the certificate and private key files that will be used for our program. In this section, we will register our Raspberry Pi 3 to AWS IoT in order to apply for AWS Greengrass.

You can follow these steps to configure Raspberry Pi 3 and other IoT devices to AWS IoT Management Console:

1. In AWS Greengrass, from the AWS IoT Management Console panel, start by clicking the **Get Started** button to define a Greengrass Group:

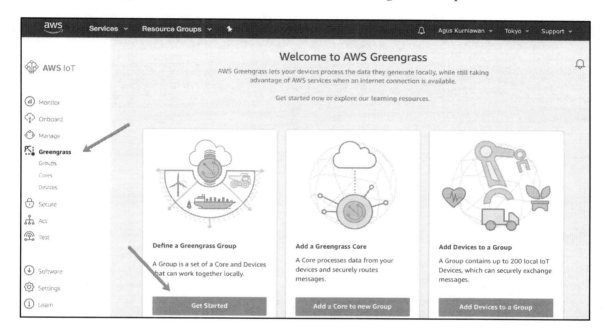

2. Select the **Easy Group creation (recommended)** option. Click on the **Use easy creation** button.
3. Fill in the Greengrass Group name. For instance, group01. When done, click on the **Next** button.
4. Then, fill in the Greengrass Core name for our Raspberry Pi 3. For instance, group01_core. When finished, click on the **Next** button.

5. You will get a confirmation about creating tasks that will be performed by AWS. If you are ready, you can start to create by clicking on the **Create Group and Core** button. This process will generate security resources for Greengrass Core and Greengrass Core software, such as certificates and key files. You can see them in the following screenshot:

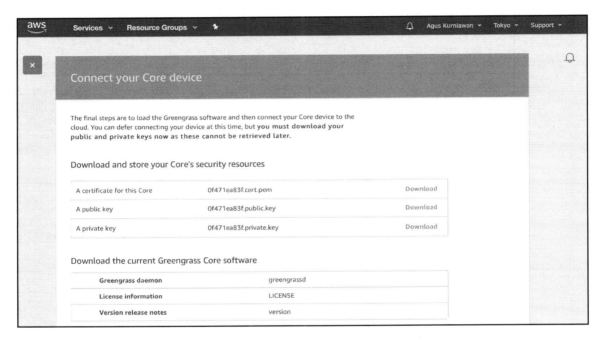

6. Download all files for the certificate, public, and private key files. Also, download Greengrass Core software, which will be deployed into our Raspberry Pi 3 board. Select **ARMv71** for the Raspberry Pi 3 board. Please click on the **Finish** button to complete all the processes.

7. To verify this, you should see our Greengrass name on the **Greengrass Groups** panel, as shown in the following screenshot:

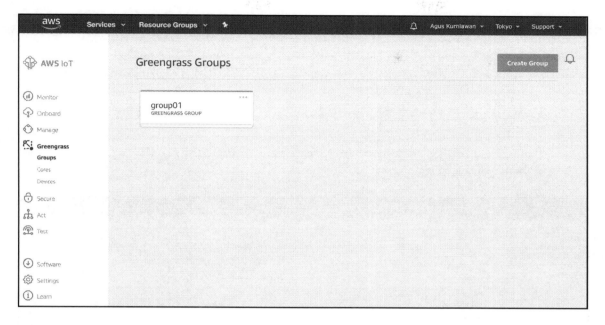

8. If you click your Greengrass Group, you should see the configuration that is shown in the following screenshot:

Configuring AWS Greengrass security

By default, AWS Greengrass can be accessed by external systems. We should configure security settings on AWS Greengrass. It's done using AWS IAM. We can create a security role for AWS Greengrass by taking the following steps:

1. Open AWS IAM Console Management on a browser with the URL `https://console.aws.amazon.com/iam`.

2. Create a role by clicking on the **Create role** button from the **Roles** menu, and you will see the following screen:

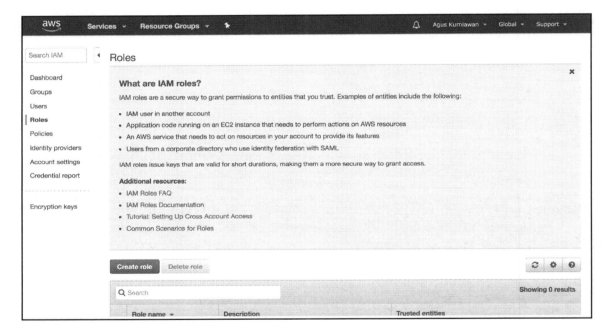

3. Select the **Greengrass** option for the service. When done, click on the **Next: Permissions** button:

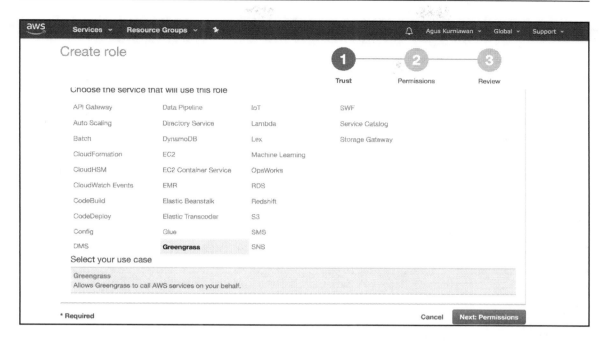

4. Fill in the role name. When finished, click on the **Create role** button:

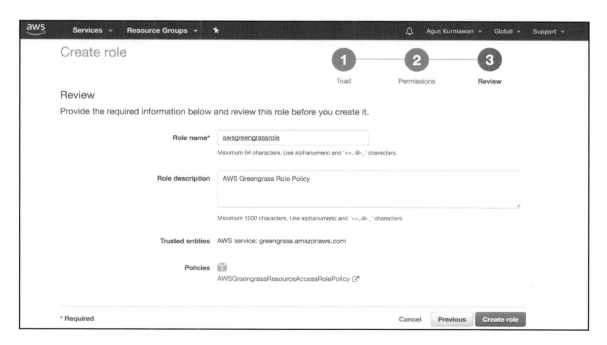

5. After the role is created, you should see it on the **Roles** panel, as shown in the following screenshot:

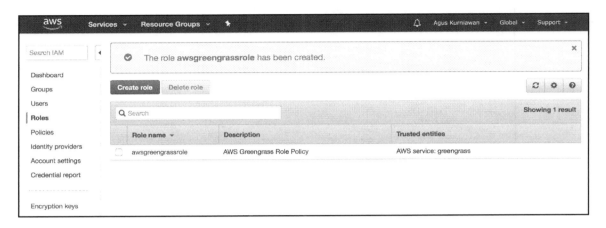

Installing AWS Greengrass on Raspberry Pi

After we have registered Raspberry Pi 3 to AWS IoT, we can install AWS Greengrass on Raspberry Pi 3. To perform the installation, Raspberry Pi 3 should be connected to the internet. Use the following steps:

1. Firstly, we configure the Lambda group in order to work with AWS Lambda. Open the /etc/fstab file:

```
$ sudo nano /etc/fstab
```

2. Then, add the following script:

```
cgroup /sys/fs/cgroup cgroup defaults 0 0
```

You can see it in the following screenshot:

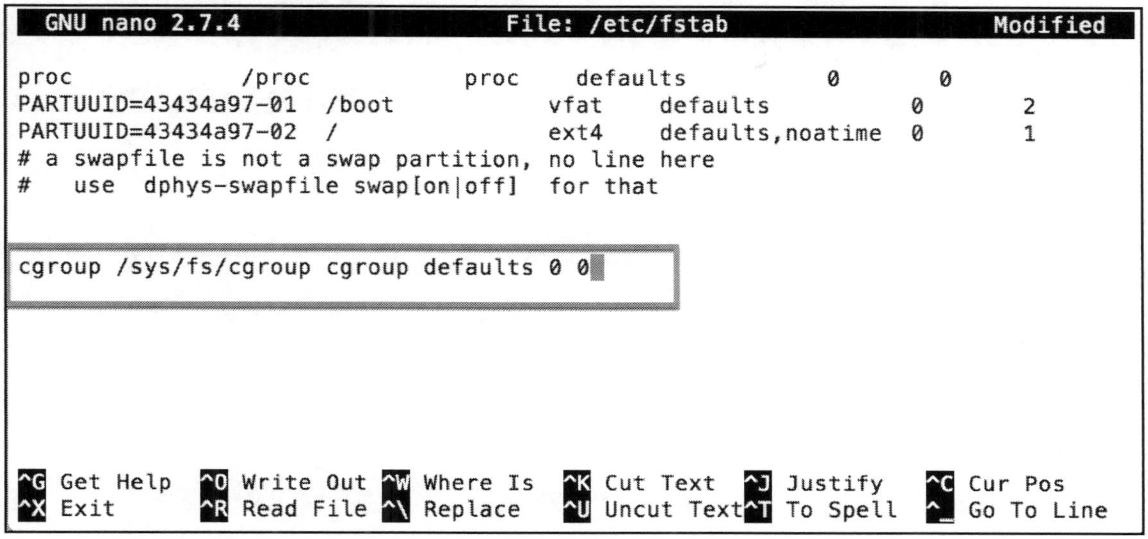

```
  GNU nano 2.7.4                    File: /etc/fstab                    Modified

proc            /proc         proc     defaults           0        0
PARTUUID=43434a97-01  /boot           vfat     defaults           0        2
PARTUUID=43434a97-02  /               ext4     defaults,noatime   0        1
# a swapfile is not a swap partition, no line here
#    use   dphys-swapfile swap[on|off]   for that

cgroup /sys/fs/cgroup cgroup defaults 0 0

^G Get Help    ^O Write Out  ^W Where Is  ^K Cut Text  ^J Justify    ^C Cur Pos
^X Exit        ^R Read File  ^\ Replace   ^U Uncut Text^T To Spell   ^_ Go To Line
```

Save this configuration.

3. In the previous section, we downloaded the Greengrass Core software file. Extract this file into a specific folder.

4. Put all the certificate files into this folder, `<extracted greengrass>/greengrass/certs`. Put the certificate file (`*.crt`), private key file (`*.key`), and AWS root certificate file into this folder. You can download the certificate files from `https://www.symantec.com/content/en/us/enterprise/verisign/roots/VeriSign-Class%203-Public-Primary-Certification-Authority-G5.pem`.

5. Then, navigate to the `<extracted greengrass>/greengrass/config` folder. You should see the `config.json` file. If not, you can create the `config.json` file. The following is the content of the `config.json` file:

```
GNU nano 2.7.4                    File: config.json

    "coreThing": {
        "caPath": "[ROOT_CA_PEM_HERE]",
        "certPath": "[CLOUD_PEM_CRT_HERE]",
        "keyPath": "[CLOUD_PEM_KEY_HERE]",
        "thingArn": "[THING_ARN_HERE]",
        "iotHost": "[HOST_PREFIX_HERE].iot.[AWS_REGION_HERE].amazonaws.com",
        "ggHost": "greengrass.iot.[AWS_REGION_HERE].amazonaws.com"
    },
    "runtime": {
        "cgroup": {
            "useSystemd": "[yes|no]"
        }
    }
}

^G Get Help   ^O Write Out  ^W Where Is   ^K Cut Text   ^J Justify    ^C Cur Pos
^X Exit       ^R Read File  ^\ Replace    ^U Uncut Text ^T To Spell   ^_ Go To Line
```

6. You can fill in the fields as follows:

- `caPath`: This is an AWS root certificate file (`*.pem`).
- `certPath`: This is a certificate file from AWS Greengrass Core (`*.crt`).
- `keyPath`: This is a private key file from AWS Greengrass Core (`*.key`).
- `thingArn`: This is the ARN from AWS Greengrass Core. You can find it at **AWS IoT | Greengrass | Cores**. You should see the thing ARN value on that web panel.
- `iotHost`: This is a hostname from AWS Greengrass Core. Just replace the `[HOST_PREFIX_HERE]` and `[AWS_REGION_HERE]` values from AWS Greengrass Core.

- ggHost: This is Greengrass endpoint. You can replace the [AWS_REGION_HERE] value for ggHost.
- useSystemd: Set this field with yes to enable cgroup.

Save this file.

7. Now you can run the Greengrass Core software. Navigate to the `<extracted greengrass>/greengrass/ggc/packages/<version>` folder. Then, type the following command:

```
$ sudo ./greengrassd start
```

8. If you are successful, you should see the Greengrass daemon being started, as shown in the following screenshot:

```
pi@raspberrypi:~/greengrass/ggc/packages/1.1.0 $ sudo ./greengrassd start
Setting up greengrass daemon
Validating execution environment
Found cgroup subsystem: cpu
Found cgroup subsystem: cpuacct
Found cgroup subsystem: blkio
Found cgroup subsystem: memory
Found cgroup subsystem: devices
Found cgroup subsystem: freezer
Found cgroup subsystem: net_cls

Starting greengrass daemon
Greengrass successfully started with PID: 801
pi@raspberrypi:~/greengrass/ggc/packages/1.1.0 $ ▮
```

Accessing AWS Greengrass

To access the AWS Greengrass server from IoT devices or other applications, we apply AWS SDK as usual. We only change our target server to the AWS Greengrass machine.

We need to build AWS Lambda into the AWS Greengrass Core machine. Then, we can access it from our IoT devices or computers. We will explore more about AWS Greengrass and IoT device interaction in the next chapter.

Building IoT projects with AWS Greengrass

In this section, we will build a simple scenario to access AWS Greengrass. We will build an AWS Lambda application into AWS Greengrass. Then, we will access it from the client application. Our scenario is illustrated in the following figure:

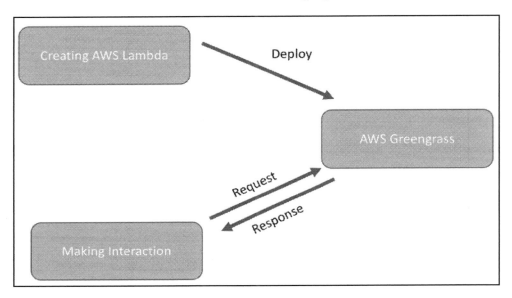

To implement this demo, we will perform the following tasks:

1. Prepare libraries on AWS Greengrass Core
2. Create AWS Lambda
3. Deploy AWS Lambda to AWS Greengrass
4. Test

Each task will be explained in the following sections.

Preparing runtime libraries on AWS Greengrass Core

The first task to ensure our AWS Lambda runs well on AWS Greengrass Core is to prepare all requirement modules/libraries. In general, we can define three modules/libraries that should be installed on the AWS Greengrass Core machine. These modules/libraries are as follows:

- AWS IoT SDK
- AWS Greengrass SDK
- External modules/libraries

AWS IoT SDK and AWS Greengrass SDK should be installed on your AWS Greengrass Core machine. You can select a runtime platform, such as Python, Node.js, or Java. Currently, AWS IoT supports Python, Node.js, and Java. You can download these libraries on AWS IoT Console:

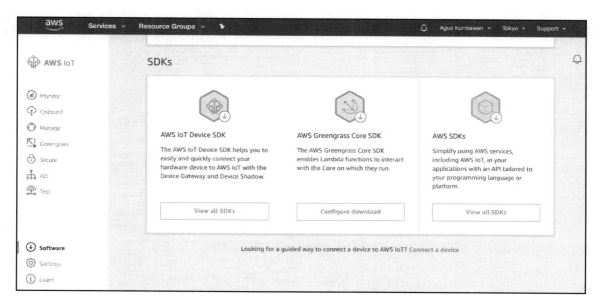

You can install the SDKs shown in the preceding screenshot. You can follow the installation guide on the web. Finally, if you use external libraries on AWS Lambda, you should install them on the AWS Greengrass Core machine too. If you have built your own libraries for Python or Node.js, then you can deploy them into Raspberry Pi.

Creating AWS Lambda

AWS Lambda is an AWS service to help you to build applications for a specific purpose. In this section, we will develop an AWS Lambda application. I will show how to develop AWS Lambda using Node.js.

Firstly, Node.js has to be installed on Raspberry Pi. Then, install AWS Greengrass Core SDK for Node.js. Based on the documentation, we should copy and paste node as nodejs6.10. You can do this with the following command:

```
$ sudo cp /usr/bin/node /usr/bin/nodejs6.10
```

```
pi@raspberrypi:~ $ node -v
v8.9.1
pi@raspberrypi:~ $ which node
/usr/bin/node
pi@raspberrypi:~ $ sudo cp /usr/bin/node /usr/bin/nodejs6.10
pi@raspberrypi:~ $
```

Prepare the Lambda program sample from AWS Greengrass Core. You can find it at <greengrass_core_sdk_js>/samples/HELLOWORLD. Inside this folder, create the node_modules folder. Copy the aws-greengrass-core-sdk folder from AWS Greengrass Core SDK for Node.js into the node_modules folder, as shown in the following screenshot:

Then, compress all files within the HELLOWORLD folder. Make sure index.js is the root of the HELLOWORLD folder. If not, AWS Lambda will not recognize your Lambda application. Finally, we have the HelloWorld.zip file that contains the Lambda application. We will upload it on AWS Lambda.

Open AWS Lambda by opening a browser and navigating to https://console.aws.amazon.com/lambda. You should see the AWS Lambda dashboard after login.

Now you can proceed with the following steps to create your AWS Lambda function:

1. Click on the **Create a function** button. You should see a form, as shown in the following screenshot:

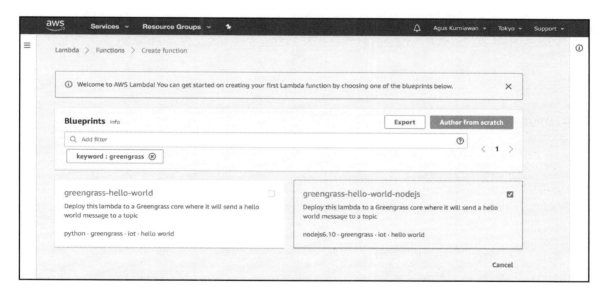

Type greengrass so you can see the application samples for Greengrass. Select **greengrass-hello-world-nodejs** by clicking on the checkbox. Then, click on the **Author from scratch** button.

2. Fill in the function and role names. Select the **Create new role from template(s)** option for the role. When done, click on the **Create function** button.

3. Now you should see the Lambda function dashboard. In the **Function code** section, select **Upload a .ZIP file** with runtime **Node.js 6.10** and **index.handler** for the handler name.

4. Click on the `HelloWorld.zip` file that we have prepared to upload the Lambda application:

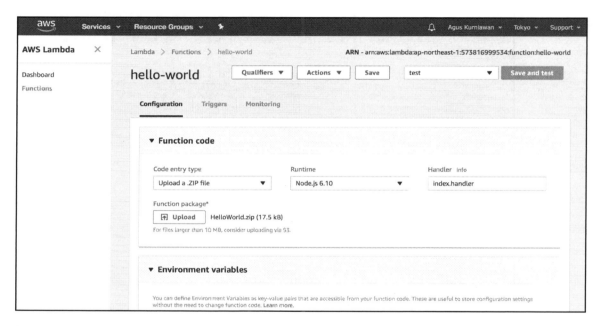

5. Then, click on the **Save** button to upload and load the Lambda program from the ZIP file. If successful, you should see Lambda program in Node.js. If it has failed, you will probably get error messages while uploading the ZIP file:

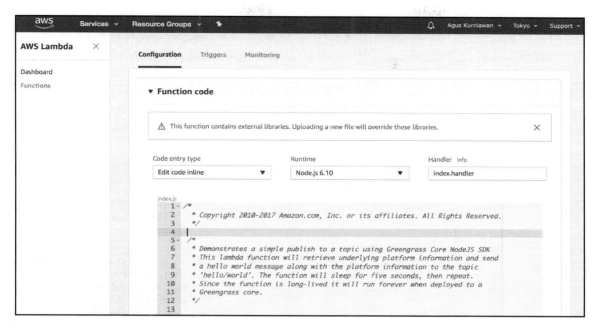

6. Now we publish this AWS Lambda. Select **Publish new version** from the **Actions** drop-down list.

7. After selecting, you should be asked to fill in the version description. Once done, click on the **Publish** button to publish AWS Lambda:

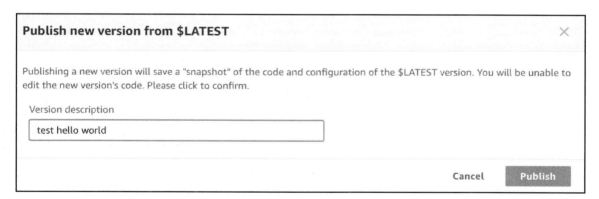

The next step is to deploy this service with our AWS Greengrass Core machine.

Deploying AWS Lambda with AWS Greengrass

After we have created AWS Lambda, we can continue to deploy AWS Lambda with AWS Greengrass. We perform the following tasks:

1. Adding Lambda to AWS
2. Configuring Lambda
3. Adding the Lambda subscription
4. Deploying to Greengrass Core

We will perform these tasks in this section:

1. Firstly, open your AWS Greengrass Group. Select the **Lambdas** menu that is shown in the following screenshot:

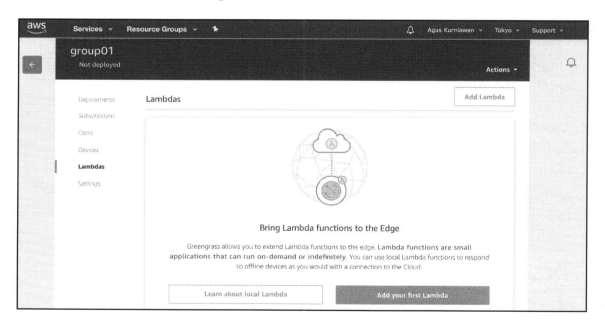

Click on the **Add Lambda** button on the upper-right side. Now you should see the Greengrass Group dashboard, as shown in the following screenshot:

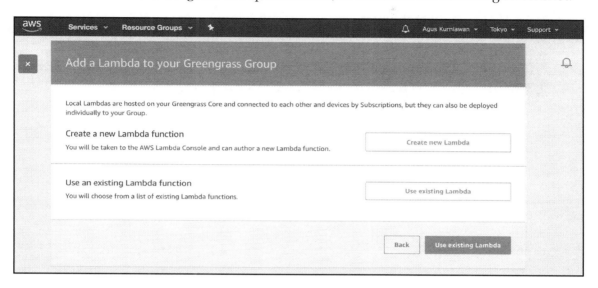

2. Select your created Lambda. Then, click on the **Next** button:

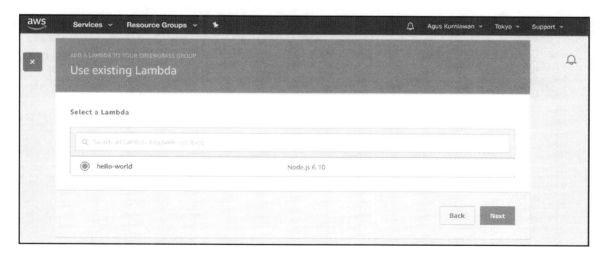

3. You will be asked for the Lambda version. Select it and click on the **Finish** button. If you succeed, you should see your Lambda on the Greengrass Group:

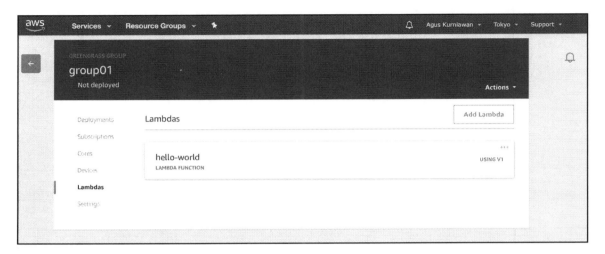

4. Now we configure our Lambda. Click on the ellipsis (...) and select the **Edit Configuration** menu, as shown in the following screenshot:

5. Select **Make this function long-lived and keep it running indefinitely** on the radio button. This option makes the Lambda function keep running indefinitely. When done, save all the changes:

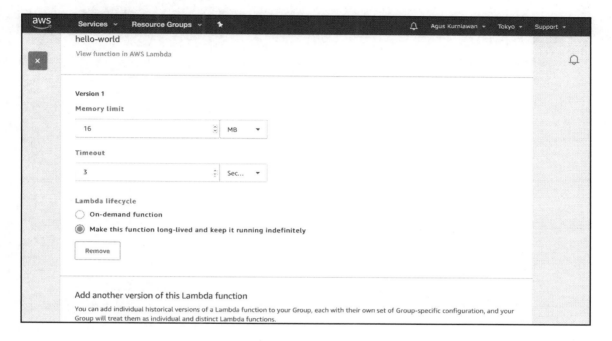

6. Now we add the subscription to access AWS Lambda. Click on the **Subscriptions** menu on the Greengrass Group. You can see it in the following screenshot:

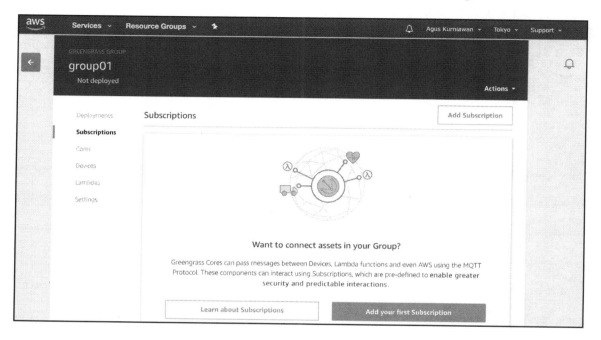

7. Click on the **Add Subscription** button to add a new subscription.
8. Fill in the source on the **Select a source** field and target on the **Select a target** field for our Lambda, as shown in the following screenshot:

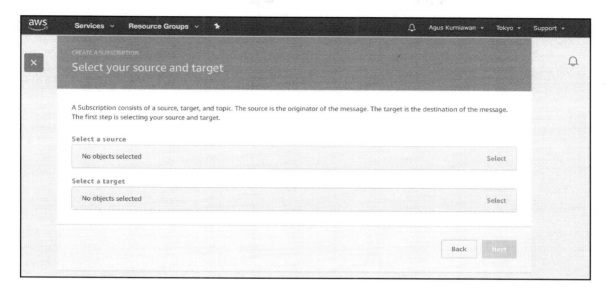

9. On the source side, click on the **Lambdas** menu. Then you select your AWS Lambda that has already been created:

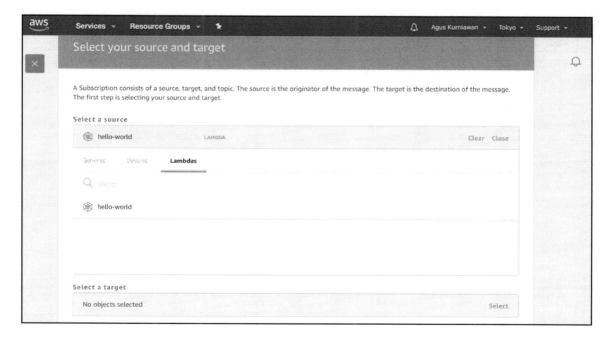

10. On the target side, you click on the **Services** section. Then select the **IoT Cloud** for targeting:

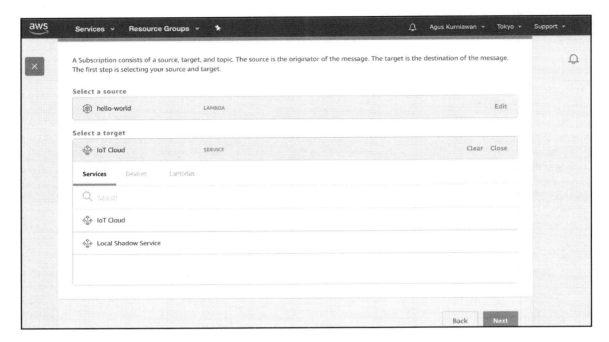

When done, click on the **Next** button.

11. Now we filter our topic. You can filter it on the **Optional topic filter** field. For instance, we set it as `hello/world`:

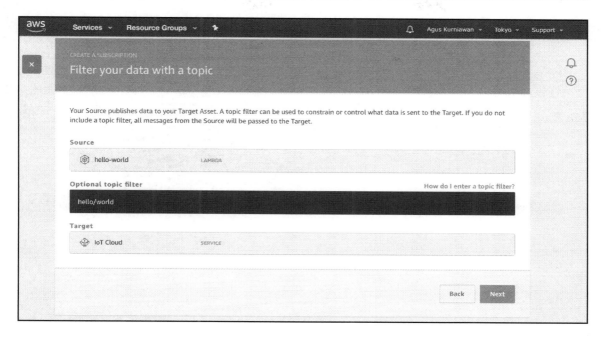

Once done, click on the **Next** button.

12. After it has been created, you can see your subscription, as shown in the following screenshot:

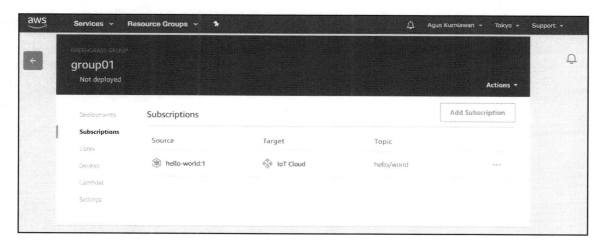

13. The last step is to deploy all the configuration to Greengrass Core. Click on the **Deployments** menu on the Greengrass Group. On the right-side of the menu, click on the **Actions** menu and select the **Deploy** option. You can see it in the following screenshot:

14. You should get the following screen. To simply configure, click on the **Automatic detection** button:

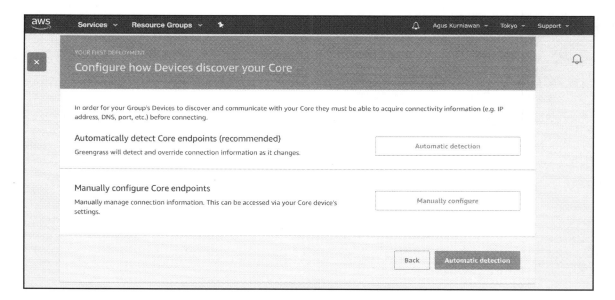

15. Then we grant permissions for other AWS services. Click on the **Grant permission** button:

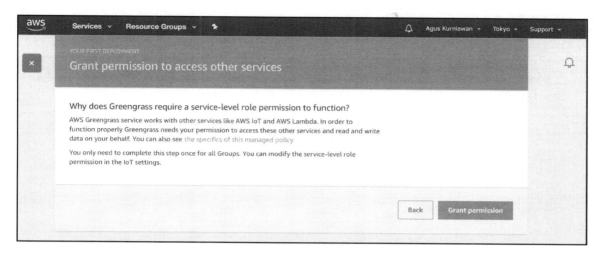

16. After that, AWS Greengrass will be deployed. You should check the deployment status. For instance, if you get a **Failed** status, as shown in the following screenshot, you should recheck your configuration. Then, try to deploy it again:

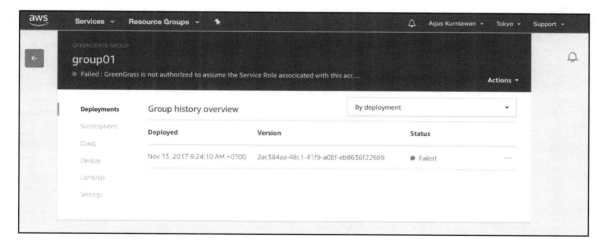

The following is a sample of a successful deployment with Greengrass Core:

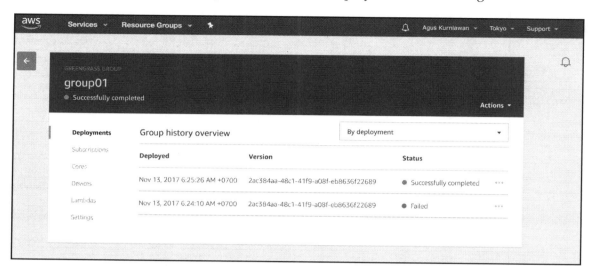

Testing Lambda from Greengrass

We can test our Lambda from Greengrass using a test tool from AWS IoT. Click on the **Test** menu. You should get a form, as shown in the following screenshot. Fill in the subscription topic that we defined while we were deploying Lambda with Greengrass Core:

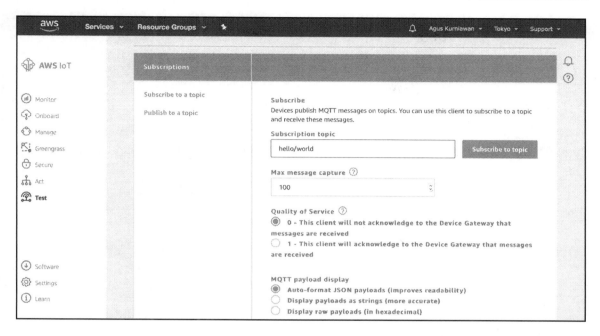

When done, click on the **Subscribe to topic** button. Now you should see messages from Raspberry Pi, as shown in the following screenshot:

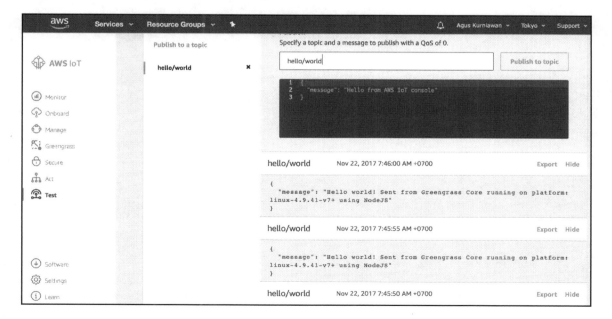

If you do not see messages from Raspberry Pi, you probably have generated errors while configuring or uploading the Lambda application.

Summary

We have learned how to deploy AWS Greengrass on the Raspberry Pi 3 board and make connectivity among IoT devices. We have also built an IoT application to connect AWS Greengrass on Raspberry Pi 3.

In the next chapter, we will learn how to build AWS Lambda on AWS Greengrass and interact with IoT devices.

4
Building Local AWS Lambda with AWS Greengrass

Extending AWS Greengrass functionalities by implementing local AWS Lambda can optimize your resources. In this chapter, we will learn how to implement AWS Lambda to local AWS Greengrass, and how it will be accessed from IoT devices. The following is a list of topics that we will cover in this chapter:

- Introducing AWS Lambda
- Deploying AWS Lambda for AWS Greengrass on Raspberry Pi 3
- Accessing AWS Lambda from IoT devices
- Building IoT projects with AWS Lambda and AWS Greengrass

Introducing AWS Lambda

AWS Lambda is one of the AWS services that provides a serverless compute to serve all the requests when executing your program. Currently, AWS Lambda for AWS Greengrass supports several program runtimes, such as Python, Node.js, and Java.

Implementing AWS Lambda into your IoT project can cut down on your infrastructure costs, especially, the cost of the server availability feature. You can focus on your problems and design your solution.

 For further information about AWS Lambda, I recommend that you read the official documentation from Amazon at `http://docs.aws.amazon.com/lambda/latest/dg/welcome.html`.

In this section, I will show you how to develop the AWS Lambda function and then invoke it. We will use the Python program to develop the AWS Lambda function and perform the following steps to implement our demo:

1. Creating the AWS Lambda function
2. Testing the AWS Lambda function
3. Publishing the AWS Lambda function
4. Configuring the AWS Lambda security
5. Invoking the AWS Lambda function

Each task will be explained in the following sections.

Creating the AWS Lambda function

In this section, we will create the AWS Lambda function by using Python. We will build the AWS Lambda function graphically through a browser. To complete this task, you should have an active AWS account:

1. Firstly, open a browser and navigate to `http://console.aws.amazon.com/lambda`. Our scenario is to build the `echo` function. It will send back any message from the caller. The message format is JSON.
2. On the AWS Lambda function dashboard, you can create a new Lambda function by clicking on the **Create function** button. Then, fill in the function name and its role, as shown in the following screenshot. When done, click on the **Create function** button. For instance, my Lambda function name is `echo-lambda`:

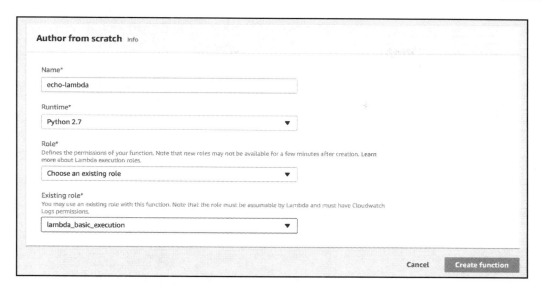

3. If successful, you will see a code editor for the AWS Lambda function. Select **Edit code inline** from the code entry type. Set **Python 2.7** for the runtime and **lambda_function.lambda_handler** for the **Handler** field. You can see this entry in the following screenshot:

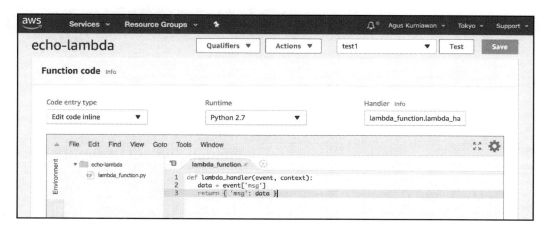

4. The following is our Python code for the AWS Lambda function. We return a message with the attribute `msg` from the caller as a JSON message:

```
def lambda_handler(event, context):
    data = event['msg']
    return { 'msg': data }
```

Save these scripts when you are done.

We have created the AWS Lambda. We will test it in the next section.

Testing the AWS Lambda function

After we have created the AWS Lambda function, we should test it before releasing it to the public. Proceed with the steps as following:

1. Click on the **Test** button to create the test scenario and you will get a screen as shown in the following screenshot:

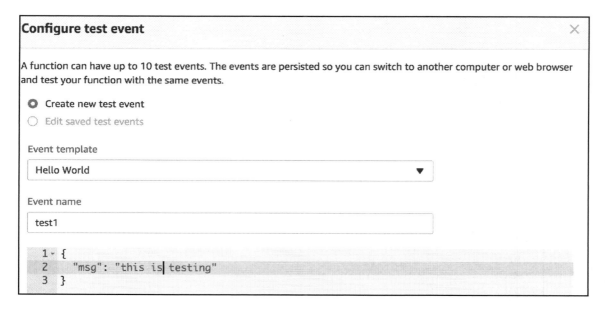

Configure test event   ×

A function can have up to 10 test events. The events are persisted so you can switch to another computer or web browser and test your function with the same events.

◉ Create new test event
○ Edit saved test events

Event template

Hello World   ▼

Event name

test1

```
1 ▾ {
2      "msg": "this is testing"
3   }
```

2. For the testing scenario, we create a data sample for testing by writing the following script:

```
{
  "msg": "this is testing"
}
```

Save this test.

3. Then we try to perform this testing by clicking on the **Test** button. If our testing is successful, we will get a positive response with a green check symbol. You can see my program output in the following screenshot:

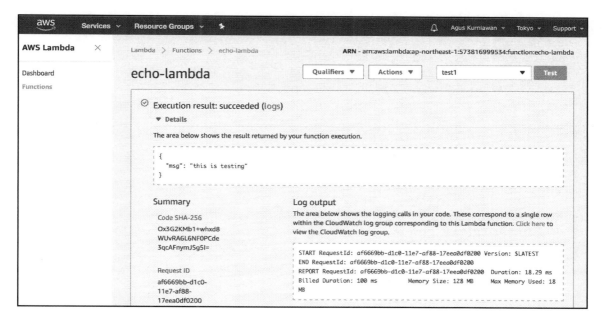

Publishing the AWS Lambda function

Now we can publish our AWS Lambda function. This is done by clicking on the **Publish new version** option on the **Actions** drop-down list. After clicking, you will get a confirmation to fill in the version description. Then, click on the **Publish** button to start publishing the AWS Lambda function:

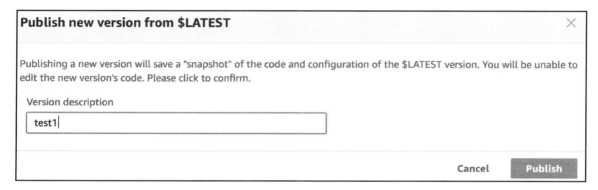

Configuring AWS Lambda security

Depending on the role setting of the AWS Lambda function, you can configure the AWS Lambda function so that it can be accessed from your account. In this section, we will configure AWS Lambda Security using AWS IAM. You can access AWS IAM through a browser and navigate to `https://console.aws.amazon.com/iam`. Add the **AWSLambdaExecute** permission on your AWS account:

Invoking the AWS Lambda function

We can invoke the AWS Lambda function from our program. For testing, we can execute from the Terminal using the AWS CLI. If you have not installed the AWS CLI yet, you can install it by following the instructions at `http://docs.aws.amazon.com/cli/latest/userguide/installing.html`:

1. For testing, we invoke our AWS Lambda with the payload `{"msg": "this is testing"}`. Type the following command:

   ```
   $ aws lambda invoke --invocation-type RequestResponse --function-
   name echo-lambda --payload '{"msg": "this is testing"}' output.txt
   ```

2. If successful, you should get the return code as `200`, as shown in the following screenshot:

```
agusk$ aws lambda invoke --invocation-type RequestResponse --function-name echo-
lambda --payload '{"msg": "this is testing"}' output.txt
{
    "StatusCode": 200
}
agusk$ nano output.txt
agusk$
```

3. To see the AWS Lambda function returning, we open the `output` file. You should see the message output as follows:

Deploying AWS Lambda with AWS Greengrass on Raspberry Pi 3

In general, we can deploy AWS Lambda with AWS Greengrass graphically and through command lines. In the previous section, we created the AWS Lambda function. In this section, will will deploy AWS Lambda with AWS Greengrass on Raspberry Pi 3.

You have learned how to deploy AWS Greengrass on Raspberry Pi in *Chapter 3, Optimizing IoT Computing Using AWS Greengrass*. Please follow the instructions in that chapter to deploy AWS Greengrass Core on Raspberry Pi.

To deploy the AWS Lambda function to AWS Greengrass Core, you should publish the AWS Lambda function and then deploy it into AWS Greengrass Group:

1. From AWS Greengrass Group, you can add the existing Lambda function that we have already created. You just select your Lambda and its version and click on **Next**. Then, select **on-demand function** for the Lambda life cycle:

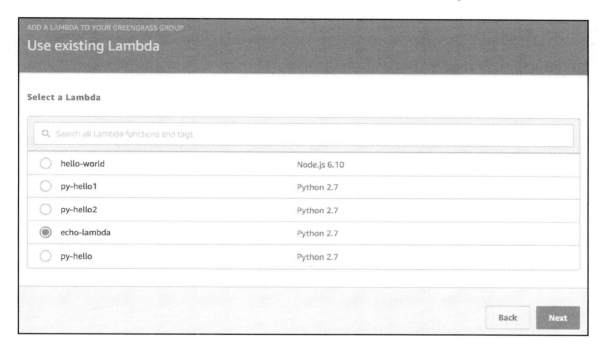

2. Furthermore, we define the subscription on AWS Greengrass. In this scenario, we add a thing, such as a computer, that will be used to invoke this Lambda. You can do it on AWS IoT Management Console.
3. You add a new subscription using the following configuration:
   - **Source**: Your thing or device
   - **Target**: Your Lambda function that you have created
   - **Topic**: test1/test2

You can see my subscriptions for the topic **test1/test2** in the following screenshot:

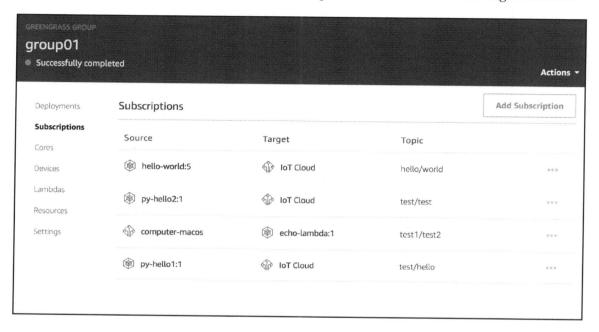

4. After completion, you can deploy this configuration into the AWS Greengrass Core machine, Raspberry Pi 3. Make sure the AWS Greengrass Core service has already started:

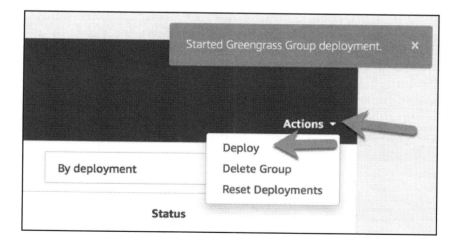

We have deployed AWS Greengrass Core. Next, we will test it by accessing from other IoT devices.

Accessing AWS Lambda from IoT devices

All API SDK for accessing AWS IoT, including AWS Greengrass, can be obtained on the software menu from AWS IoT Management Console. You can install it based on your device and runtime platforms.

In this section, I will show you how to invoke Lambda from AWS Greengrass Core. For testing, I used the Node.js application. You should install the `aws-sdk` library for Node.js. You also need to access the key ID and secret access key from the AWS IAM.

Please write the following complete program:

```
var AWS = require('aws-sdk');
AWS.config.update({region:'<region>'});

var accessKeyId = '<accessKeyId>'
var secretAccessKey = '<secretAccessKey>';
AWS.config.update({accessKeyId: accessKeyId, secretAccessKey:
secretAccessKey});

var lambda = new AWS.Lambda();
var params = {
 FunctionName: '<lambda-function-arn>',
 Payload: '{"msg": "this is testing"}'
};
lambda.invoke(params, function(err, data) {
 if (err) console.log(err, err.stack);
 else console.log(data);
});
```

Now you can run the preceding program using the following command:

```
$ node lambda_invoker.js
```

On successful execution, you should see a message on the Terminal that shows the status and response message from Lambda. A sample of the program output can be seen in the following screenshot:

```
agusk$ node lambda_invoker.js
{ StatusCode: 200,
  ExecutedVersion: '$LATEST',
  Payload: '{"msg": "this is testing"}' }
agusk$
```

We have accessed AWS Lambda from an IoT device or computer. You can do more experiments to get experience with AWS Lambda.

Next, we will integrate AWS Lambda with other AWS services.

Building IoT projects with AWS Lambda and AWS Greengrass

Integrating AWS Lambda and AWS Greengrass can leverage your IoT business. In this section, we will explore IoT projects to implement AWS Lambda and AWS Greengrass. We will build a simple app to monitor a local resource, such as a sensor.

Accessing local resources

AWS Greengrass can access local resources. This is possible if we use AWS Greengrass version 1.3.0 or later versions. You can configure an AWS Lambda to access specific resources. The following is a list of local resources that you can apply:

- Folders and files
- Serial ports
- USB
- GPIOs
- GPUs
- Cameras

To show you how to work with local resources in the AWS Greengrass Core machine, we will access local GPIO resources. We need an LED that is attached to Raspberry Pi on GPIO 18 (pin 12). You can see this wiring in the following image:

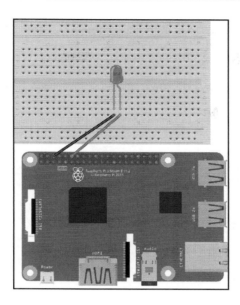

Our aim is to develop a blinking Lambda. This demo will make a blinking LED while the Lambda function is called. The next step is to develop AWS Lambda and then configure the AWS Greengrass Core machine.

Developing local AWS Lambda

We use Node.js to develop local AWS Lambda. Firstly, we write the Node.js program with the Raspberry Pi environment. Open the Raspberry Pi Terminal and create a folder called `blinking`. We will use the `node-rpio` library to access the Raspberry Pi GPIO. This library can be found at `https://github.com/jperkin/node-rpio`.

1. Navigate to the `blinking` folder from the Terminal. Then, we install the `node-rpio` library by typing the following command:

   ```
   $ npm install rpio
   ```

2. You also need to configure AWS Lambda to enable working with `gpiomem`. You can do that by typing the following command:

   ```
   $ sudo cat >/etc/udev/rules.d/20-gpiomem.rules <<EOF
   SUBSYSTEM=="bcm2835-gpiomem", KERNEL=="gpiomem", GROUP="gpio",
   MODE="0660"
   EOF
   ```

3. Now, create the `index.js` file to write our blinking program. You can write this complete program for the `index.js` file as follows:

```javascript
const ggSdk = require('aws-greengrass-core-sdk');
var rpio = require('rpio');

const iotClient = new ggSdk.IotData();
const os = require('os');
const util = require('util');

function publishCallback(err, data) {
 console.log(err);
 console.log(data);
}

...

setTimeout(greengrassBlinkingdRun, 2000);

exports.handler = function handler(event, context) {
 console.log(event);
 console.log(context);
};
```

4. Compress the `index.js` file included in the `node_modules` folder into a file called `blinking.zip`. Now you can upload the `blinking.zip` file into AWS Lambda Management Console.

Since this Lambda function accesses local resources, this Lambda cannot perform Lambda testing on AWS Lambda Management Console. You should only perform publishing directly.

Explanation: The following program will call the `greengrassBlinkingRun()` function once. Inside the function, it will open GPIO 18 (12 pin) and write the `;HIGH/LOW` value into the GPIO. The program will also publish a message using the `publish()` function:

```javascript
function greengrassBlinkingdRun() {
 rpio.open(12, rpio.OUTPUT, rpio.LOW);
 rpio.write(12, rpio.HIGH);
 iotClient.publish(pubOpt, publishCallback);
 rpio.sleep(1);

rpio.write(12, rpio.LOW);
 state = rpio.LOW;
 iotClient.publish(pubOpt, publishCallback);
 rpio.sleep(1);
```

```
    rpio.close(12);
}
setTimeout(greengrassBlinkingdRun, 2000);
```

Configuring AWS Greengrass Core

After we have published AWS Lambda, we can consume this Lambda function into AWS Greengrass. Firstly, we need to prepare our resources for the local AWS Greengrass Core.

Follow these steps to configure local resources on AWS Greengrass Core:

1. Open AWS Greengrass Group and then add new local resources from the **Resources** menu. Fill in the resource name; for instance, GPIO. Select the **Device** option for **Local resource type** with the /dev/gpiomem path, as shown in the following screenshot:

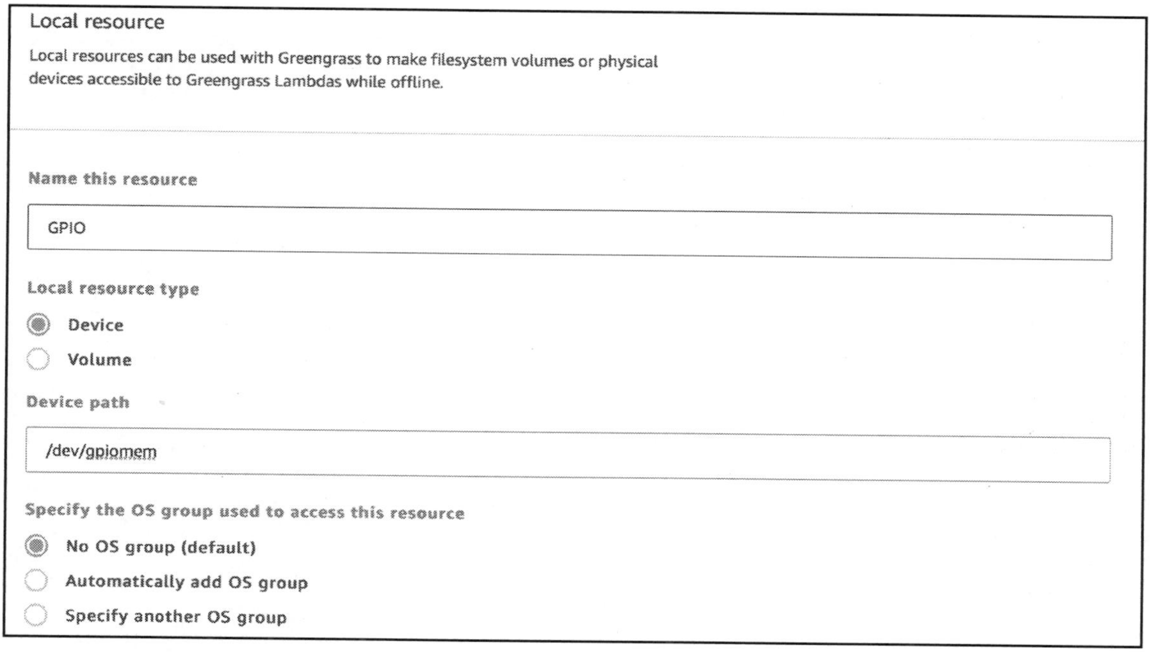

Local resource

Local resources can be used with Greengrass to make filesystem volumes or physical devices accessible to Greengrass Lambdas while offline.

Name this resource

> GPIO

Local resource type

◉ Device

◯ Volume

Device path

> /dev/gpiomem

Specify the OS group used to access this resource

◉ No OS group (default)

◯ Automatically add OS group

◯ Specify another OS group

Save this resource.

2. Now, create Lambda on AWS Greengrass Group from the existing Lambda that we have already created. After this Lambda is created, you can add our GPIO resource. You can enable the **Read access to /sys directory** option to ensure our Lambda can access local resources.

3. You should also add a new subscription for our local Lambda. Set the source from our local Lambda and target for the IoT Cloud. You can set any topic, for instance, pi/blinking.

4. Before deploying to AWS Greengrass Core, you should configure your Raspberry Pi 3. Regarding the security issue, you should configure ggc_user as a member of the GPIO group. Please execute the following command on the Raspberry Pi Terminal in order to configure ggc_user as the member of gpio:

```
$ sudo adduser ggc_user gpio
```

If not configured, you will probably get problems, as shown in the following screenshot:

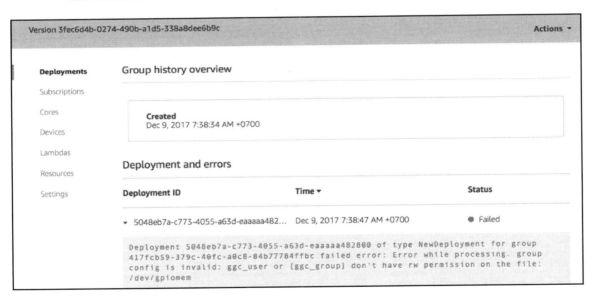

5. Reboot your Raspberry Pi 3 and then start the Greengrass service after the reboot is completed.

Now you can deploy AWS Greengrass into the AWS Greengrass Core machine.

Testing the demo

You can run this demo using the **Test** website from AWS IoT Management Console. You can set it to subscribe with `pi/blinking`. You should see the blinking LED once.

Interacting with things within a group

In this section, we will develop an application to interact between IoT devices within the AWS Greengrass Group. This feature enables our IoT devices to consume resources from other IoT devices. To work with this case, we should register all IoT devices in the AWS IoT Management Console. Then, add those IoT devices into AWS Greengrass Group.

We can access an IoT board within one group from AWS Greengrass Core. AWS IoT can interact with IoT boards through AWS Greengrass Core. You can see this in the following figure:

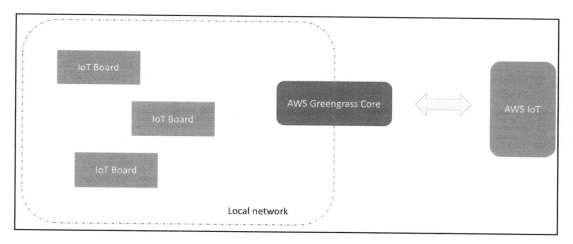

For a demo, we will develop publisher and subscriber applications to show how those IoT devices communicate with each other. For testing, we use a sample program from AWS IoT Python SDK at `https://github.com/aws/aws-iot-device-sdk-python`.

1. Firstly, add at least two IoT devices into the current AWS Greengrass Group. Then, on the **Subscriptions** menu, add a new subscription.

2. Select the source for any IoT device name and target for the other IoT device name. Set the subscription topic, for instance, `sensor/hello`. You can see this in the following screenshot:

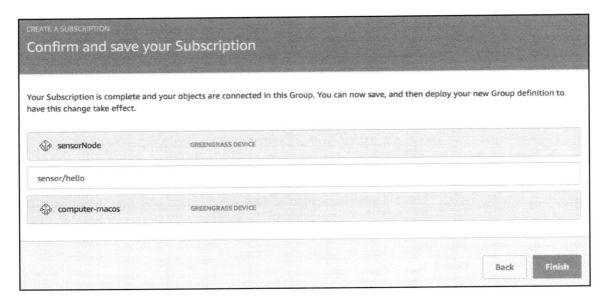

3. Download all the certificates and private key files from your IoT devices and save them into one folder. You should install AWS IoT Python SDK on your IoT devices. In this case, it is my computer. You can install this SDK using the following command:

```
$ pip install AWSIoTPythonSDK
```

4. Now you can download a sample program from `https://github.com/aws/aws-iot-device-sdk-python/blob/master/samples/greengrass/basicDiscovery.py`. Then, save it into one folder with our IoT device certificate and key files:

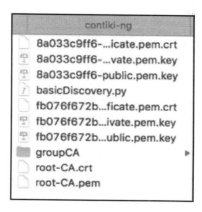

contiki-ng
8a033c9ff6-...icate.pem.crt
8a033c9ff6-...vate.pem.key
8a033c9ff6-public.pem.key
basicDiscovery.py
fb076f672b...ficate.pem.crt
fb076f672b...ivate.pem.key
fb076f672b...ublic.pem.key
groupCA
root-CA.crt
root-CA.pem

5. Now you can open the Terminal and run the publisher program as follows:

```
python basicDiscovery.py -e host_aws_greengrass_core -r root-
CA.pem -c iotdevice1-certificate.pem.crt -k iotdevice1-
private.pem.key -n iotdevice1-name -m publish -t 'sensor/hello'
-M 'This message from sensorNode'
```

Here:

- `host_aws_greengrass_core` is the hostname or name from the AWS Greengrass Core machine
- `root-CA.pem` is the certificate file for AWS
- `iotdevice1-certificate.pem.crt` is a certificate file from IoT device 1
- `iotdevice1-private.pem.key` is a private key from IoT device 1
- `iotdevice1-name` is the IoT device 1 name
- `sensor/hello` is the subscription topic
- `This message from sensorNode` is a message sample

6. Furthermore, we run a program for the subscriber application as follows:

```
python basicDiscovery.py -e host_aws_greengrass_core -r root-
CA.pem -c iotdevice2-certificate.pem.crt -k iotdevice2-
private.pem.key -n computer-macos -m subscribe -t
'sensor/hello'
```

Here:

- `host_aws_greengrass_core` is the hostname or name from the AWS Greengrass Core machine
- `root-CA.pem` is the certificate file for AWS
- `iotdevice2-certificate.pem.crt` is a certificate file from IoT device 2
- `iotdevice2-private.pem.key` is a private key from IoT device 2
- `iotdevice2-name` is the IoT device 2 name
- `'sensor/hello'` is the subscription topic

On successful execution, you should see a message that is sent and received by the programs, as shown in the following screenshot:

Summary

We have learned how to work with local Lambda on AWS Greengrass. We also developed programs to access local resources and communicate between IoT devices.

In the next chapter, we will learn how to work AWS IoT Button and apply it in your IoT projects.

5

Expanding IoT Capabilities with AWS IoT Button

Amazon provides a one-click solution through AWS IoT Button hardware. This solution enables an interaction between the AWS platform and other IoT devices. In this chapter, we will learn how to work with AWS IoT Button and build an IoT application applying AWS IoT Button.

The following is a list of topics that we will explore in this chapter:

- Introducing AWS IoT Button
- Reviewing the project scenario for AWS IoT Button
- Setting up AWS IoT Button
- Interacting between AWS IoT Button and IoT devices
- Building your IoT project with AWS IoT Button

Introducing AWS IoT Button

AWS IoT Button is one of the AWS services that interacts with the AWS backend. AWS IoT Button is built based on the Amazon Dash Button hardware. This device provides connectivity capability through Wi-Fi to communicate with the AWS server.

The first AWS IoT Button hardware appeared in October of 2015. The current AWS IoT Button hardware is the second generation. You can buy this hardware on Amazon's website at https://www.amazon.com/All-New-AWS-IoT-Button-Generation/dp/B01KW6YCIM. You can also check it on your local Amazon website.

The AWS IoT Button form can be seen in the following image. It consists of a button and indicator LED. AWS IoT Button can detect users pressing in the following three types:

- Single clicked
- Double clicked
- Long clicked

Each clicked type can be connected to a specific action. AWS IoT Button can also be integrated with other AWS services, such as AWS IoT and AWS Lambda.

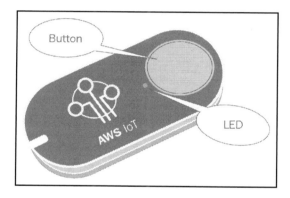

Reviewing a project scenario for AWS IoT Button

If you search for Dash Button on the Amazon website, you will see various Dash Buttons that are provided by companies to serve certain business services. These scenarios could probably inspire you to implement AWS IoT Button in a real environment:

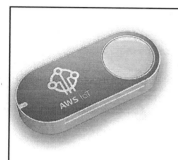

All-New AWS IoT Button (2nd Generation)
by Amazon

$19⁹⁵ ✓prime
FREE Shipping on eligible orders

 ▾ 28

Product Features
... Things, based on the Amazon *Dash button* hardware, the AWS IoT button ...

Cascade Dash Button
by Amazon

$4⁹⁹ ✓prime
Exclusively for Prime Members

Product Features
... Amazon *Dash Button* is a Wi-Fi connected device that reorders your ...

For instance, we can connect our AWS IoT Button to a smart home. While you click the button, you can turn on all the lamps in your home. In addition, you can connect AWS IoT Button for safety scenarios; for instance, the button will call the police while it is being clicked. You can see this scenario in the following figure:

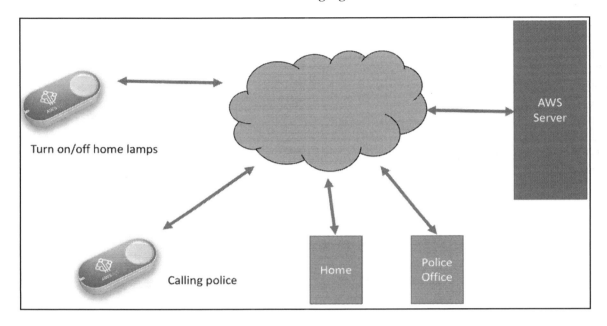

The idea of AWS IoT Button revolves around what your system will do if AWS IoT Button is clicked. There are a lot of scenarios that you can see in your environment.

Setting up AWS IoT Button

In this section, we are going to set up AWS IoT Button. Assume you have a second generation, or later, AWS IoT Button. If you don't have AWS IoT Button hardware, you can buy it from Amazon's website. You also need a Wi-Fi hotspot with a supported internet connection.

In general, we can set up AWS IoT Button by performing the following steps:

1. Register AWS IoT Button to AWS IoT
2. Connect AWS IoT Button to a network
3. Test the connectivity

Each step will be presented in the following sections.

Registering AWS IoT Button to AWS IoT

To set up your AWS IoT Button, we should register it on AWS IoT Management Console. Since AWS IoT Button can be treated as a thing, we can perform this registration through a browser with the URL `https://console.aws.amazon.com/iot`. Please refer to `Chapter 4`, *Building Local AWS Lambda with AWS Greengrass*, to register a thing, namely AWS IoT Button.

On successful registration of the button, we will obtain a certificate and public and private key files that we need to upload to AWS IoT Button in the next section.

Connecting AWS IoT Button to a network

In this section, we will connect our AWS IoT Button to a network. Consider the following steps:

1. Firstly, press the button on the AWS IoT Button hardware until you see a blinking blue LED on the hardware. Then, you should see SSID Wi-Fi from AWS IoT Button, with the name **Button ConfigureMe - xxx**:

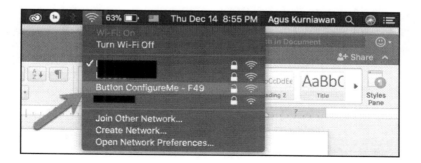

2. To connect to the AWS IoT Button Wi-Fi, you should enter the SSID pin which is eight digits. You can find it on the back of AWS IoT Button, as shown in the following screenshot. Take eight digits from the back, for instance `1234KL34`. Remove the space:

3. After connection, you can open a browser and navigate to `http://192.168.0.1/index.html`. You should see the screen that is shown in the following screenshot:

Button ConfigureMe

Enter the value for any field that you wish to change for device: G030PT020437PKCK

Wi-Fi Configuration:

SSID	▨▨▨▨▨ ◈ ⬅
Security	☐ Open Network (No Password)
Password	2▨▨▨▨▨▨ ⬅

AWS IoT Configuration:

Certificate	Choose File 📄 2ebff44fd3-...ate.pem.crt ⬅
Private Key	Choose File 🔑 2ebff44fd3-...ate.pem.key ⬅
Endpoint Subdomain	▨▨▨▨▨▨
Endpoint Region	ap-northeast-1 ◈
Final Endpoint	▨▨▨▨▨.iot.ap-northeast-1.amazonaws.com

☑ By clicking this box, you agree to the <u>AWS IoT Button Terms and Conditions</u>.

Configure

4. Fill in your existing SSID and its pin. You also need to upload the certificate and private key files that you obtain while registering AWS IoT Button. You need to fill in the **Endpoint Subdomain** and **Endpoint Region** fields. To find **Endpoint Subdomain**, you can see your AWS IoT endpoint on AWS IoT Management Console. Click on the **Settings** menu. You should see the AWS IoT endpoint on AWS IoT Management Console.

We have now configured AWS IoT Button. Your AWS IoT Button can access AWS IoT now.

You also can configure your AWS IoT Button through mobile applications. For Android, you can download it at `https://play.google.com/store/apps/details?id=com.amazonaws.iotbuttonhl=en` and iOS at `https://itunes.apple.com/us/app/aws-iot-button/id1178216626?mt=8`.

Testing

Now you can test your AWS IoT Button using the MQTT client from AWS IoT. Perform the following steps:

1. Click on the **Test** menu and then fill in the subscriber topic, **iotbutton/+,** and click on the **Subscribe** button.
2. Once done, you can test it by clicking on your AWS IoT Button. Once the button is pressed, you will see a blinking white LED. This means that AWS IoT Button is sending data to AWS IoT. After data transmission to AWS is completed, our MQTT client can see the message `"message": "Hello from AWS IoT console"`, as seen in the following screenshot. Try to perform a double click on AWS IoT Button. It should show `"DOUBLE"` on `clickType` from message:

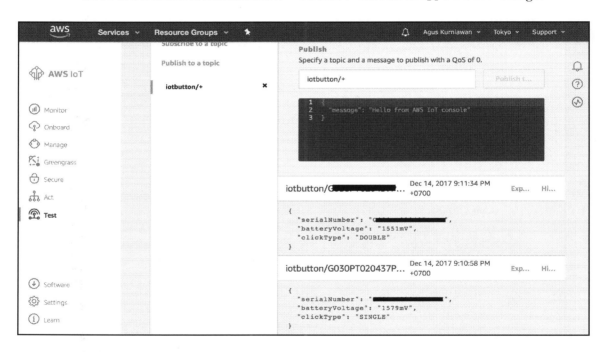

Interaction between AWS IoT Button and IoT devices

We have learned how to communicate with AWS IoT Button. In this section, we will continue developing the IoT application to enable interaction between IoT devices and AWS IoT Button. Our scenario is to apply Raspberry Pi 3 with the attached LED. When AWS IoT Button is clicked, the LED will be lit. Otherwise, the LED will be turned off if AWS IoT Button is double clicked. You can see this scenario in the following image:

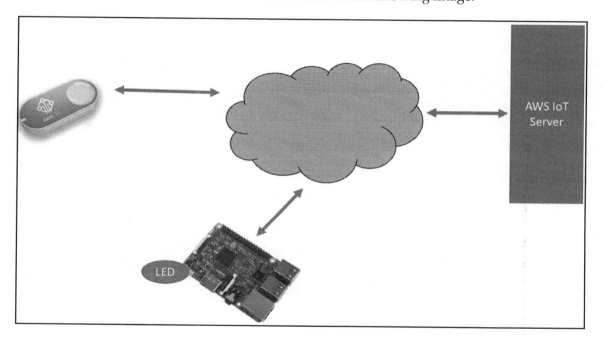

To enable accessing AWS IoT from Raspberry Pi 3, you should register it to obtain a certificate, private, and public keys files. We will use them to access the AWS IoT server. We use the same wiring from Chapter 4, *Building Local AWS Lambda with AWS Greengrass*. We attach the LED on GPIO 18 (pin 12), as seen in the following image:

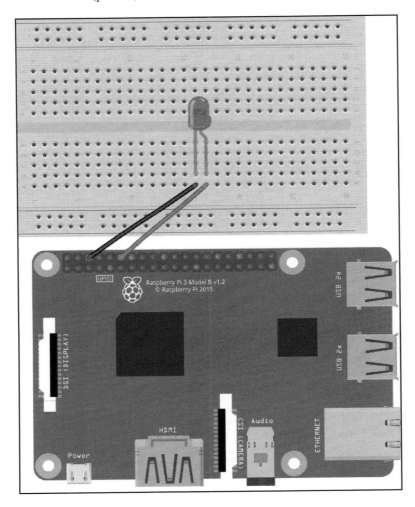

For program implementation, we use the Node.js platform. We should install AWS IoT SDK for Node.js. We also need the `rpio` library to access GPIO that we learned in `Chapter 4`, *Building Local AWS Lambda with AWS Greengrass*.

The Node.js application will subscribe a topic, **iotbutton/+,** and listen to the incoming message. Once you have clicked on AWS IoT Button, the button type of AWS IoT Button shows `SINGLE`. The program will turn on the LED. Otherwise, if we click twice on AWS IoT Button, we obtain the `DOUBLE` clicked type. The program will turn off the LED.

We use the previous program for the publisher/subscriber. We only modify on the subscriber topic. Then, we filter the clicked type from the incoming message. The following is a code snippet for the Node.js application:

```
var awsIot = require('aws-iot-device-sdk');
var rpio = require('rpio');

...

device
  .on('message', function(topic, payload) {
  console.log('message', topic, payload.toString());

  var ret = JSON.parse(payload.toString());
  if(ret.clickType=='SINGLE'){
  console.log('SINGLE clicked --> TURN ON LED');
  rpio.open(12, rpio.OUTPUT, rpio.LOW);
  rpio.write(12, rpio.HIGH);
  }
  if(ret.clickType=='DOUBLE'){
  console.log('DOUBLE clicked --> TURN OFF LED');
  rpio.open(12, rpio.OUTPUT, rpio.LOW);
  rpio.write(12, rpio.LOW);
  }
});

...

});
```

You should change `keyPath` for the private key file and `certPath` for the certificate file from Raspberry Pi 3. Save this program as the `aws-iot-pi.js` file.

You can run this program using the following command in Raspberry Pi 3:

```
$ node aws-iot-pi.js
```

Now you can test by clicking the button once and also by double clicking it. You should obtain incoming messages and on/off lighting. A sample of the program output can be seen in the following screenshot:

```
pi@raspberrypi:~/Documents/iot-button $ node aws-iot-pi.js
connected
Waiting commmands..
message iotbutton/█████████████ {"serialNumber": "███████████████", "battery
Voltage": "1656mV", "clickType": "SINGLE"}
SINGLE clicked --> TURN ON LED
message iotbutton/█████████████ {"serialNumber": "███████████████", "battery
Voltage": "1619mV", "clickType": "DOUBLE"}
DOUBLE clicked --> TURN OFF LED
```

While testing, my Raspberry Pi 3 shows the LED being lit after IoT is clicked once in the following image:

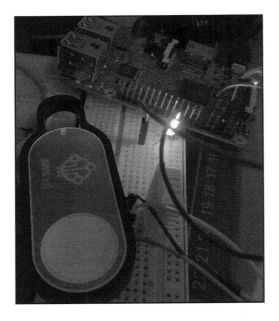

Building your IoT project with AWS IoT Button

We will continue to develop IoT projects using AWS IoT Button. We will use the Lambda rule and trigger to perform a certain action. For the demo, we save a message from AWS IoT Button into the AWS database, DynamoDB.

You can see this scenario in the following figure. Each button clicked from AWS IoT Button will be filtered and then call AWS Lambda. Inside AWS Lambda, the program will store a message into the database, AWS DynamoDB:

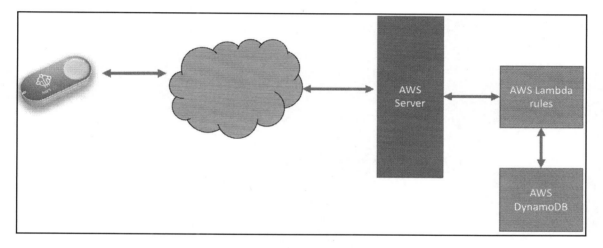

Configuring AWS DynamoDB

Firstly, we create a table on AWS DynamoDB. You can open a browser and navigate to https://console.aws.amazon.com/dynamodb. Then, you can create a new table. For instance, we set the table name as aws-iot-button-db. We also set the primary key as msg-id with the **String** data type. You can see the AWS DynamoDB table configuration in the following screenshot:

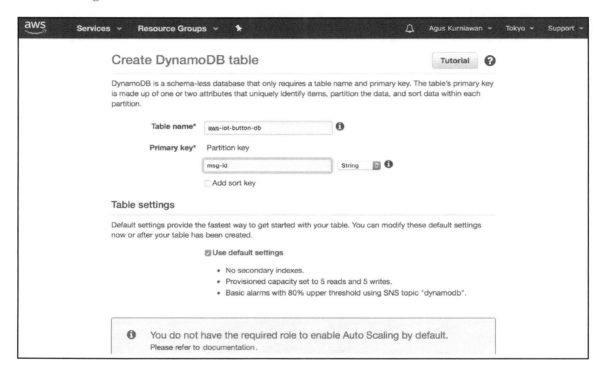

With this we have successfully created AWS DynamoDB on Amazon AWS. Next, we will connect it with AWS Lambda.

Building Lambda and its rule

After we have created a table on AWS DynamoDB, we can continue developing the AWS Lambda function. We will use Node.js runtime to write the program for AWS Lambda. Just navigate to `https://console.aws.amazon.com/lambda` from your browser. We will create the AWS Lambda function from scratch:

1. Fill in your Lambda function name; for instance, `aws-iot-button`. Select Node.js for runtime and your existing role or create a new one if you don't have one. The Lambda role is important to ensure your Lambda has permission to access AWS DynamoDB. I will explain it in the last section:

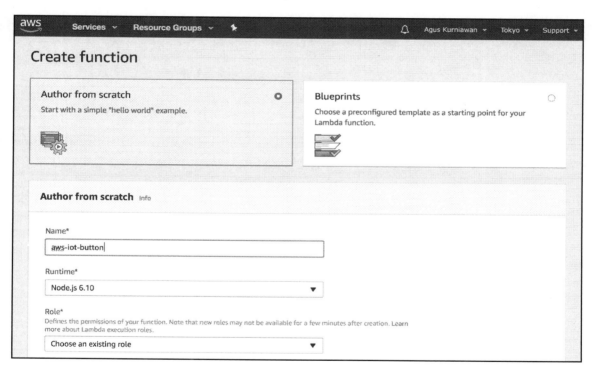

2. On your Lambda function dashboard, we develop a trigger to filter incoming messages from AWS IoT Button. Click on the **Configuration** section and select **AWS IoT** to add a new trigger, as shown in the following screenshot:

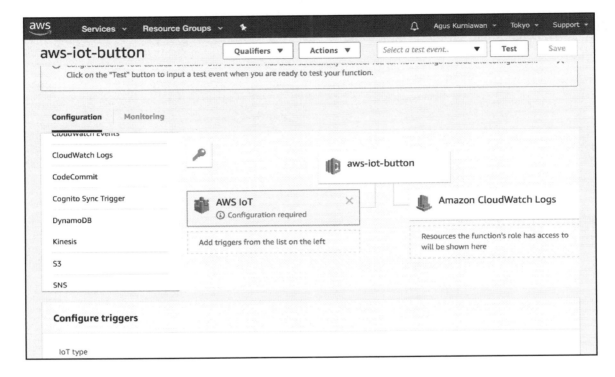

3. On the **Configure triggers** panel, you select **IoT Button** for the IoT type. Fill in your AWS IoT Button hardware serial **Device Serial Number (DSN)**. You can find it on the back of the hardware. Then, click on the **Generate certificate and keys** button to download the certificate:

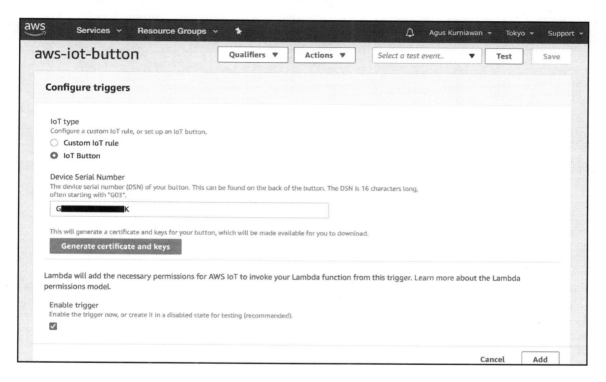

Certificate and private key files should be uploaded to the AWS IoT Button hardware. You can do this task by referring to the explanation in the previous section.

4. As I have stated regarding the Lambda role, we should configure it on https:// console.aws.amazon.com/iam/. Select the **Roles** menu. Then, find the role name that is assigned on our AWS Lambda. Open it and you will see it on the **Permissions** tab.

5. You should have **AmazonDynamoDBFullAccess** on the policy list. If not, please add the **AmazonDynamoDBFullAccess** policy into your role:

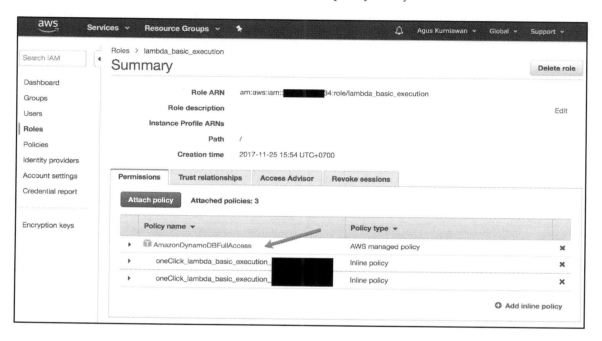

We have configured the AWS Lambda role in order to access AWS DynamoDB. Next, we will write a program for AWS Lambda

Building a Lambda program

We will build a Lambda function to filter an AWS IoT Button message. This message is parsed on an event from the handler function. To store a message into AWS DynamoDB, we use the `putItem()` function from the `DynamoDB` object with the passing JSON message.

The following is the complete program for the AWS Lambda function:

```
var AWS = require('aws-sdk');
var ddb = new AWS.DynamoDB();

exports.handler = (event, context, callback) => {

  var params = {
  TableName: 'aws-iot-button-db',
  Item: {
  'msg-id': {S:new Date().getTime().toString()},
  'CLICKED' : {S:event.clickType},
  'BUTTON_ID' : {S:event.serialNumber},
  }
  };

  // Call DynamoDB to add the item to the table
  ddb.putItem(params, function(err, data) {
  if (err) {
  callback(err, 'Error');
  } else {
  callback(null, 'Success');
  }
  });
};
```

Once done, please save all the programs.

We are done writing a program for AWS Lambda. Next, we will test it using AWS IoT Button.

Testing using IoT Button

Now you can test by clicking on AWS IoT Button once or twice. Then, you can verify these messages on AWS DynamoDB. When you click once on AWS IoT Button, you should see the SINGLE message on the CLICKED column on the aws-iot-button-db table from AWS DynamoDB. Otherwise, if you click twice on AWS IoT Button, you should get the DOUBLE message on AWS DynamoDB.

You can see all incoming messages on the **Items** tab, as shown in the following screenshot:

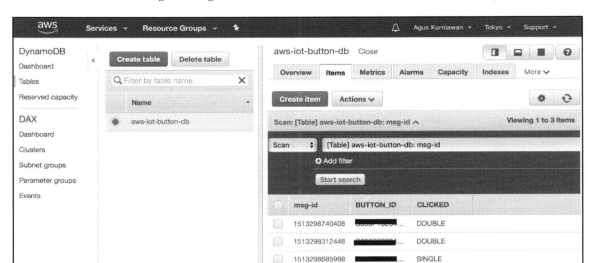

Summary

We have now learned how to work with AWS IoT Button. We saw how to interact with IoT devices, such as Raspberry Pi 3. We also developed an IoT program, applying other AWS services.

In the next chapter, we will learn how to visualize IoT data on an AWS service.

6
Visualizing AWS IoT Data

Some sensor data, as a result of sensing from IoT devices, is probably stored in a database engine. Getting insightful data from the IoT sensor data is more interesting when focusing on your business continuity. In this chapter, we will learn how to work with sensor data and visualize it in order to easily read and obtain insightful data.

The following is a list of topics that we will explore in this chapter:

- Introducing IoT massive data
- Introducing brief data visualization
- Data visualization in the web
- Consuming real-time sensor data in web applications
- Visualizing data from AWS IoT
- Introducing Amazon QuickSight
- Consuming sensor data from Amazon QuickSight
- Building data visualization for your IoT projects

Introducing IoT massive data

These days, there is a lot of data we can find from various sources. Customer profiles, e-commerce transactions, sensor data from IoT, and social media are massive data. Regarding the data from IoT, Gartner reported that *8.4 billion connected things were used in 2017*. For more information, refer to `https://www.gartner.com/newsroom/id/3598917`. Gartner predicts that connected things, such as IoT devices, will reach 20.4 billion by 2020.

As we know, there are a lot of new IoT platforms to implement IoT projects. These boards can generate sensor data. Each data has its own data type that represents sensor information, such as temperature and humidity.

The following figure illustrates that data comes from any source, such as sensor, transaction, social media, news, email, and medical. This data is regarded as massive data in the internet era:

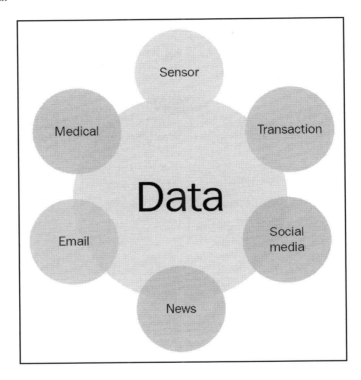

Introducing brief data visualization

Data visualization is designed to present data in a graphical style. We can obtain more insight data from the data visualization result. For instance, we have temperature data from sensor measurements, as depicted in the following table. Sensor Data-Temperature is a value from the temperature sensor device:

No	Sensor Data-Temperature
1	20
2	21
3	22
4	23
5	24
6	24
7	25
8	25
9	26
10	27
11	28
12	27
13	27
14	26
15	24
16	23
17	22
18	21
19	20
20	19

We can see the temperature value at a certain hour. From this data, we can visualize the graph, as shown in the following image:

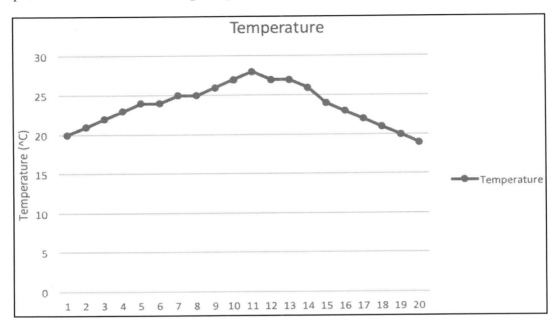

Comparing visualizing data in the table to the graph seems to show that we can get more insight if we present our data in the form of graphs. In this chapter, we will focus on how to visualize sensor data in a graphical format.

Data visualization in the web

Most people use web applications to perform their business or to present their data to customers. There are a lot of web application frameworks that we can use to develop. Corresponding to IoT data, we can apply web applications to visualize our data.

In this section, we will review some JavaScript frameworks to visualize IoT data. I will not review all the frameworks but I will start with three JavaScript frameworks in order to inspire you to use data visualization.

Data-Driven Documents (D3)

D3.js is a JavaScript library for manipulating documents based on data. D3.js has a large number of community members. It supports HTML, SVG, and CSS. Officially, you can get more information about D3.js at `https://d3js.org`. You can get source code for this library at `https://github.com/d3/d3`.

For the demo, we will develop the web program using Dj3. library. The program will display data using the Dj3 library. You can follow these steps to perform the demo:

1. In general, you should download the D3.js file from `https://github.com/d3/d3/releases`. Then, you can include it in your web application, as follows:

   ```
   <script src="libs/d3.js"></script>
   ```

2. You can also include the D3.js file from the CDN server using the following script:

   ```
   <script src="https://d3js.org/d3.v4.min.js"></script>
   ```

3. For the demo, we can visualize the sensor data in JSON format. The following is a sample of the JSON data:

   ```
   [
   { "x": 1, "y": 10},
   { "x": 10, "y": 10},
   { "x": 20, "y": 10},
   { "x": 30, "y": 30},
   { "x": 40, "y": 32},
   { "x": 50, "y": 35},
   { "x": 55, "y": 40},
   { "x": 60, "y": 25},
   { "x": 70, "y": 70},
   { "x": 80, "y": 80},
   { "x": 90, "y": 20},
   { "x": 100, "y": 80}
   ]
   ```

   Save this data as the `data.json` file. This data will be retrieved from the web application using jQuery, so you should download the jQuery file from `http://jquery.com`.

4. Now you can create a simple HTML file, called d3demo.html. Firstly, we declare the D3.js and jQuery files (d3.js and jquery-3.2.1.js), including the HTML style within the <script> tag:

```
...

<meta charset="UTF-8">
<title>D3.js Demo</title>
<script src="libs/d3.js"></script>
<script src="libs/jquery-3.2.1.js"></script>
<style>
.axis path, .axis line
{
fill: none;
stroke: #777;
shape-rendering: crispEdges;
}

...

.bar
{
fill: FireBrick;
}
</style>
</head>
```

5. Inside the HTML body, we insert our chart canvas by declaring the svg attribute. We set the width and height as 500 and 250 pixels, respectively. We will generate a chart using JavaScript scripts:

```
<body>
<svg id="img" width="500" height="250"></svg>

<script language="JavaScript">
 // visualize data

</script>
</body>
</html>
```

6. To generate a chart using D3.js, we call $.getJSON() to get the JSON data. Then, we call the display_data() function to generate a chart. Consider the following code snippet:

```
$(document).ready(function() {
$.getJSON('data.json', function(data) {
console.log(data);
display_data(data);
});
})

function display_data(sensorData) {
 var vis = d3.select("#img"),
 WIDTH = 500,
 HEIGHT = 250,
 MARGINS = {
 top: 20,
 right: 20,
 bottom: 20,
 left: 50
 },
 ...
yRange = d3.scaleLinear()
 .range([HEIGHT - MARGINS.top, MARGINS.bottom])
 .domain([d3.min(sensorData, function (d) {
 return d.y;
 }),
 d3.max(sensorData, function (d) {
 return d.y;
 })
 ]),
 ...
vis.append("svg:path")
 .attr("d", lineFunc(sensorData))
 .attr("stroke", "blue")
 .attr("stroke-width", 2)
 .attr("fill", "none");

}
```

All D3.js APIs can be found at `https://github.com/d3/d3/wiki`. In this demo, we display the data in the `line` object. Save the HTML file. You can put this HTML file into a browser. You should see a graphical format to visualize the data, as shown in the following screenshot:

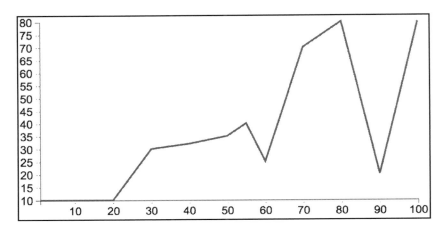

You have have now learned how to use the D3.js library to visualize data on a web application.

Chart.js

Chart.js is a very light charting library for creating responsive charts using HTML/HTML5 canvas elements. In my opinion, this library is easier to use. You can read and download the Chart.js file at `http://www.chartjs.org`. You can download the Chart.js library at `https://github.com/chartjs/Chart.js`.

For the demo, we will develop a web application to visualize data using the Chart.js library. To show how to use the Chart.js in web application, we will use the same JSON data from the previous section to visualize the data. You can follow these steps to perform the demo:

1. Create an HTML file, called `chartjs.html`. Then, put the Chart.js file and jQuery files into the HTML header:

```
<!DOCTYPE html>
<html lang="en">
<head>
 <meta charset="UTF-8">
 <title>Chart.js Demo</title>
```

```
<script src="libs/Chart.js"></script>
<script src="libs/jquery-3.2.1.js"></script>
</head>
```

2. To render a chart, we define the canvas on the HTML body. In this scenario, we define the width and height for our canvas as 200 and 100 pixels, respectively. We will generate a chart using JavaScript scripts:

```
<body>
<canvas id="myChart" width="200" height="100" style="border:1px
solid #000000;"></canvas>
<script>
 // generate a chart

</script>
</body>
</html>
```

3. We use the Chart object with the line type. You can read about this API at http://www.chartjs.org/docs/latest/charts/line.html. The following is the implementation program to generate a chart:

```
$(document).ready(function() {
$.getJSON('data.json', function(data) {
console.log(data);
show_data(data);
});
});

 function show_data(data){
    var ctx =
document.getElementById("myChart").getContext('2d');
   var myLineChart = new Chart(ctx, {
       type: 'line',
       data: {
        datasets: [{
         label: 'Sensor data',
         borderColor: "rgba(210, 54, 54, 1)",
         fill: false,
         data: data
        }]
       },
       options: {
        scales: {
           xAxes: [{
           type: 'linear',
           position: 'bottom'
```

```
    }]
  }
}
});
}
```

4. Save this file. Then, run that HTML file into your web server. You can see my chart program in the following screenshot:

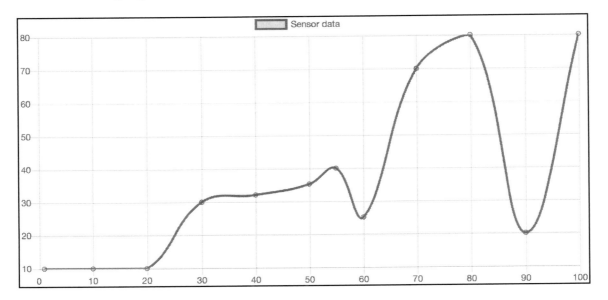

We have learned how to work with the Chart.js library to visualize data on a web application.

Flot

Flot is a plotting library for jQuery, with a focus on simple usage, attractive looks, and interactive features. This library provides some plugins to extend your cases. The Flot library can be found at http://www.flotcharts.org. Some Flot files are shown in the following screenshot:

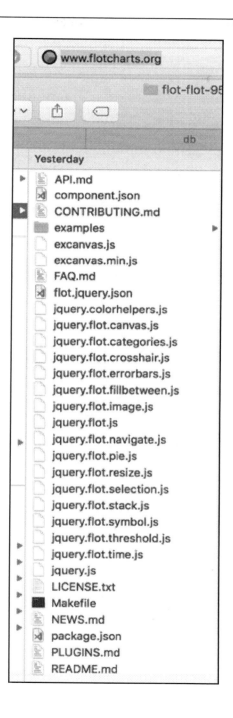

For the demo, we will visualize random data using the Flot library on web applications. You can follow these steps to perform the demo:

1. For testing, we create an HTML file, `flotdemo.html`. Firstly, we put jQuery Flot and jQuery into a HTML header. You can also define styles for your web:

```html
<!DOCTYPE html>
<html lang="en">
<head>
 <meta charset="UTF-8">
 <title>Flot Demo</title>
 <script src="libs/jquery-3.2.1.js"></script>
 <script src="libs/jquery.flot.js"></script>
 <style>
 #placeholder
 {
 width: 100%;
 height: 500px;
 }
 </style>
</head>
```

2. In the HTML body, we will generate a chart into the `div` attribute with the `placeholder` ID using the JavaScript scripts:

```html
<body>
<div id="placeholder"></div>
<script language="JavaScript">
 // generate a chart
</script>
</body>
</html>
```

3. In this demo, we generate data from the `sin` math formula. Then, we insert data from the `Flot` object:

```javascript
$(document).ready(function() {
    show_data();
});
function show_data(){
   var d1 = [];
   for (var i = 0; i < 14; i += 0.5) {
     d1.push([i, Math.sin(i)]);
   }

   $.plot("#placeholder", [{
```

```
        data: d1,
        lines: { show: true, fill: true }
    }]);
}
```

4. Save this HTML file. Then, you can run that into the web server so you should see a graphic in the browser, as shown in the following figure:

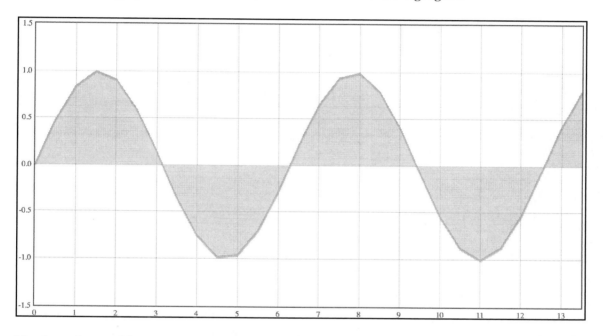

You have learned how to work with the Flot library on a web application to visualize data.

Now you have already learned how to visualize data with three libraries, D3.js, Chart.js, and Flot. All the data is static data. Next, we will visualize the progressive data, such as real-time sensor data.

Consuming real-time sensor data in a web application

In this section, we will learn how to visualize sensor data in real time. The scenario is to perform sensing from an IoT device and then send sensor data to the client app. This concept is similar to the publisher/subscriber application. This scenario is depicted in the following figure:

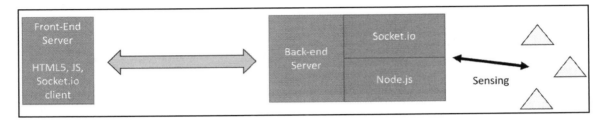

To implement how to visualize sensor data in real time, we will develop a web application that utilizes HTML5 and JavaScript. Once the sensing process is done, the sensor data will be sent to the web client application. The data pushing engine can apply the **Socket.IO** library to address data transferring in real time.

Socket.IO provides a JavaScript/Node.js that implements WebSocket to push data from the backend to the frontend. This library can serve request sensor data and push the data. You can get more information about Socket.IO at `https://socket.io/`.

In this section, we will develop a web application using Node.js and apply Express for the web framework. You can read more information about the Express framework at `http://expressjs.com`. This framework will handle HTTP GET/POST requests.

Now you can follow these steps to perform the demo:

1. To develop Node.js, we install Socket.IO and Express on our project. You should have already installed Node.js on your platform. You can open a Terminal and type the following commands:

   ```
   $ mkdir sensor
   $ cd sensor/
   $ npm init
   ```

   These commands will create a folder, named `sensor`. Then, generate the `package.json` file for all library configurations.

2. Now you can install the `express` and `socket.io` libraries into your project. Type these commands:

```
$ npm install express --save
$ npm install --save socket.io
```

Your machine should be connected to the internet in order to install these libraries.

3. The next step is to create `index.js` for the Node.js application. The program, `index.js`, will serve all the HTTP requests, including Socket.IO requests. The following is the `index.js` program implementation:

```
var express = require('express');
var app = express();
var http = require('http').Server(app);
var io = require('socket.io')(http);

app.use(express.static('public'));

app.get('/', function(req, res){
  res.sendFile(__dirname + '/index.html');
});

io.on('connection', function(socket) {
  var dataPusher = setInterval(function () {
    socket.broadcast.emit('data', Math.random() * 100);
  }, 1000);

  socket.on('disconnect', function() {
    console.log('closing');
  });

});

http.listen(3000, function(){
  console.log('listening on *:3000');
});
```

In this program, the sensor data is generated by the random value. The program will listen on port 3000.

4. Next, we create a folder, named `public`. Insert all the HTML, JS, and CSS files. This demo will use the Flot library to visualize sensor data. Furthermore, put the jQuery and Flot files into the `public/js` folder.

5. You also should create `index.html` within the `public` folder. `index.html` will act as frontend application that requests sensor data through Socket.IO. You can see the project structure in the following screenshot:

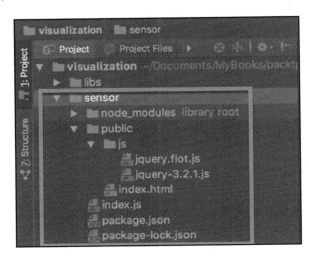

The `index.html` file will perform Socket.IO requests to retrieve sensor data. The following is the program implementation for the `index.html` file:

```html
<html>
<head>
    <meta http-equiv="Content-Type" content="text/html;
charset=utf-8">
    <title>Visualizing Real-Time Sensor Data</title>
    <script language="javascript" type="text/javascript"
src="/js/jquery-3.2.1.js"></script>
    <script language="javascript" type="text/javascript"
src="/js/jquery.flot.js"></script>
    <script src="/socket.io/socket.io.js"></script>
    <script language="javascript" type="text/javascript">
        var socket = io.connect();
        var items = [];
        var counter = 0;
        socket.on('data', function (data) {
            items.push([counter, data]);
            counter = counter + 1;
            if (items.length > 20)
```

```
            items.shift();
        $.plot($("#placeholder"), [items]);
    });
</script>

</head>
<body>
<h1>Real-Time Sensor Data Visualization</h1>
<br>
<div id="placeholder" style="width:600px;height:300px;"></div>
</body>
</html>
```

Save this program.

6. To run the program, you can execute it by typing the following command:

   ```
   $ node index.js
   ```

7. After execution, open the browser and navigate to `http://localhost:3000`.
   You should see a graph in the browser, displaying real-time data from the server.
   A sample of the web application can be seen in the following screenshot:

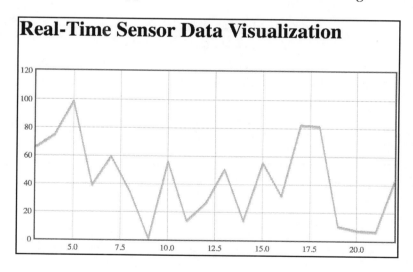

Visualizing data from AWS IoT

In the previous section, we learned how to visualize data from the backend server that was built from Node.js. In this section, we will continue to work with data visualization. Now we will consume sensor data from AWS IoT. We will develop a simple project to consume sensor data from AWS IoT and then visualize it in the browser environment.

Our demo scenario can be described in the following figure. We develop the Node.js application that performs sensing of the physical environment, such as temperature and humidity. You can use a sensor device, such DHT11 and DHT22. For this demo, I will generate random values for the temperature sensor:

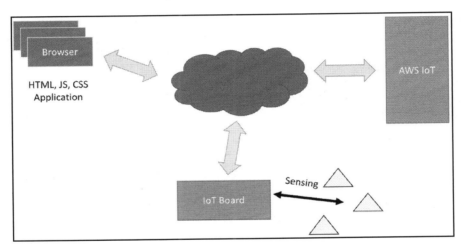

The sensor data will be sent to AWS IoT with the publisher/subscriber model approach. We can use AWS IoT SDK for JavaScript/Node.js to send data to AWS IoT on a specific topic channel. Furthermore, we will implement a client application-based on web application. We will create a simple web application using HTML5 and JS to retrieve sensor data from AWS IoT.

To implement our demo, we will perform some steps in order to run the project. The following is a list of steps that we will apply:

- Configuring AWS IoT
- Configuring AWS Cognito
- Configuring AWS IAM
- Developing a sensor publisher
- Developing data visualization from AWS IoT
- Running the project

Each step will be performed in the following sections:

Configuring AWS IoT

The first step to implement this project is to configure AWS IoT. Each IoT device that wants to access AWS IoT should be registered so that we can obtain a certificate and key files. This step is required. Otherwise, you will get an error while your device sends data to AWS IoT.

We have learned how to configure AWS IoT from the previous chapters. In this demo, we need at least one registered IoT device on AWS IoT. After you have registered, you should have a certificate, public, and private key files. You also need the AWS certificate file. Please read the previous chapters to perform this task. This IoT device is used to send the data to AWS IoT. This scenario can also be called a **sensor data publisher**. You can see my registered IoT devices in the following screenshot

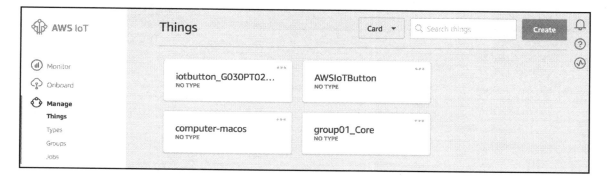

Configuring AWS Cognito

Amazon Cognito is one of the AWS services that provides an identity federation. Amazon Cognito enables third-party apps to access AWS resources. We will use Amazon Cognito, which will be applied for the web application in order to enable access to AWS IoT resources, such as sensor data. We should add an identity pool in Amazon Cognito. It will be used in our web application to access sensor data from the AWS IoT.

1. To configure Amazon Cognito, you can open the browser and navigate to `https://console.aws.amazon.com/cognito/`. You should get the following screen:

2. Next, we create an identity pool by clicking on the **Manage Federated Identities** button. Then, you can create a new identity pool, as shown in the following screenshot:

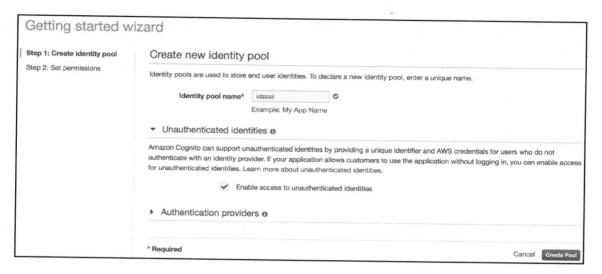

Fill in the name of your identity pool and check the **Enable access to unauthenticated identities** checkbox. Once done, click on the **Create Pool** button.

3. Next, you should give permission to your pool identity in order to access AWS resources. You can click on the **View Details** section, as shown in the following screenshot:

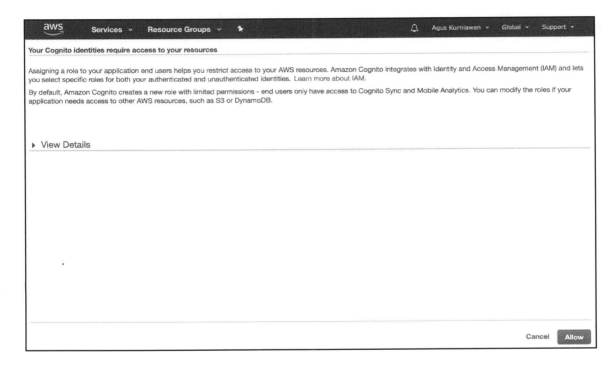

4. In this scenario, we do not change anything. Click on the **Allow** button to give permission to access AWS resources:

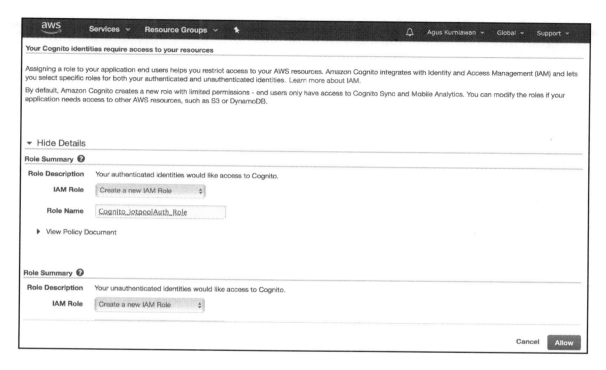

5. You have now created an identity pool. You should see the identity pool dashboard, as shown in the following screenshot:

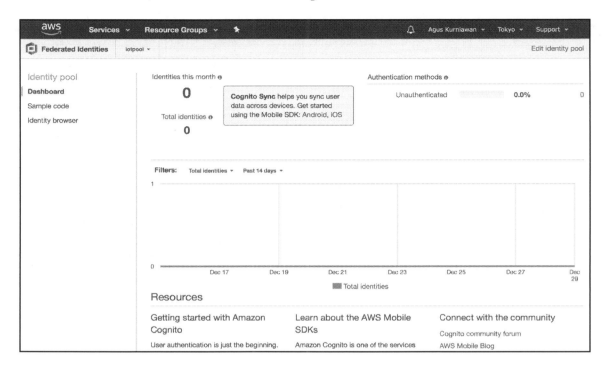

6. Now, you should copy your identity pool ID and role name for the unauthenticated role. These values are shown in the following screenshot. Copy these values and we will use them for our web application and AWS IAM configuration:

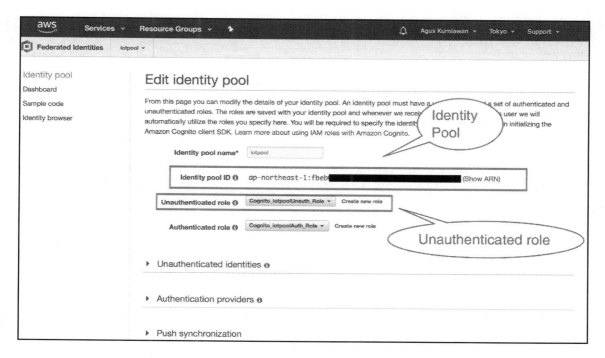

Finally, we have successfully configured AWS Cognito. Now, we will configure AWS IAM for security accesses in the next section.

Configuring AWS IAM

When we create an identity pool, we have an unauthenticated role in the result. This role should be configured on AWS IAM in order to access AWS IoT.

1. Open the browser and navigate to `https://console.aws.amazon.com/iam/`. You should get the AWS IAM dashboard. Select **Roles** on the left menu. Find your unauthenticated role name that is used by your identity pool.

2. On the role summary from the identity pool for the unauthenticated role, you should add the **AWSIoTDataAccess** policy. To do that, you can click on the **Permissions** tab. Then, click on the **Attach policy** button. Find the **AWSIoTDataAccess** policy and check it, as shown in the following screenshot:

3. Click on the **Attach policy** button once done.

4. You should see the **AWSIoTDataAccess** policy in your identity role, as shown in the following screenshot:

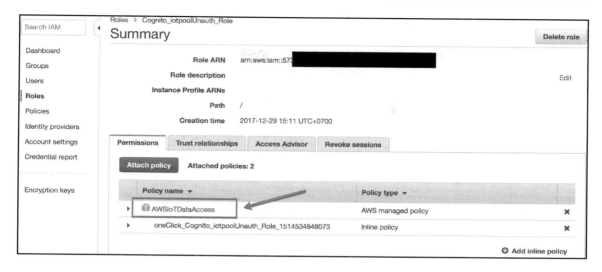

Now your identity pool can access AWS IoT data resources. Next, we will develop a sensor publisher application to send sensor data to AWS IoT.

Developing a sensor publisher

In this section, we will develop a sensor publisher. A sensor publisher is a system that generates sensor data and then perform to publish that sensor to a certain server. We can implement this application by using Node.js. Ensure your computer has Node.js installed. A sensor publisher will send sensor data at certain periods. For the demo, I generated a random value between 10 and 35 for the temperature sensor. Consider the following steps:

1. Firstly, we create a folder named `sensor-publisher` and initialize the project using `npm init`:

```
$ mkdir sensor-publisher
$ cd sensor-publisher/
$ npm init
```

2. Then, we install AWS IoT SDK for JavaScript/Node.js. For this, type the following command:

```
$ npm install aws-iot-device-sdk --save
```

3. Insert the certificate and private key files from the IoT device that have been obtained from AWS IoT. Moreover, we continue to write the program. Create a file, sensor-publisher.js. Write the following complete program in this file:

```javascript
var awsIot = require('aws-iot-device-sdk');

var device = awsIot.device({
keyPath: 'xxxx-private.pem.key',
certPath: 'xxxx-certificate.pem.crt',
caPath: 'root-CA.pem',
host: '<host>.iot.<region>.amazonaws.com',
clientId: 'user-testing',
region: '<region>'
});

device
.on('connect', function() {
 console.log('connected to AWS IoT.');

 setInterval(function(){
 // random 10 - 35
 var data = {
 'temperature': Math.floor((Math.random() * 35) + 10)
 };
 device.publish('iot/sensor', JSON.stringify(data));
 console.log('sent: ', JSON.stringify(data));
 }, 3000);
});

console.log('Sensor publisher started.');
```

In the preceding code, change the following values:

- keyPath is the private key from the IoT device
- certPath is the certificate file from the IoT device
- caPath is the certificate file for AWS IoT
- <host> is the hostname for AWS IoT
- <region> is a region name for your AWS

This program will send data on the `iot/sensor` topic every 3 seconds. To send data to AWS IoT, we call the `device.publish()` function. Sensor data is built in JSON format; for instance, a sample of sensor data in JSON:

```
{ 'temperature': 23 }
```

In the next section, we will develop a frontend application, web app, to consume sensor data from AWS IoT.

Developing data visualization from AWS IoT

In this section, we will create a web application to consume sensor data. We will implement the program using HTML5 and JS. Technically, the HTML5 application will communicate with AWS IoT using MQTT over HTTP. This is done if we use AWS IoT SDK for JavaScipt/Node.js and AWS SDK.

1. Firstly, we create a folder; for instance, `aws-iot-visualz`. Then, we initialize the Node.js project by creating the `package.json` file. Type the following commands:

   ```
   $ mkdir aws-iot-visualz
   $ cd aws-iot-visualz/
   $ npm init
   ```

2. Next, we install the required libraries for Node.js. We need the following libraries:
   - AWS IoT SDK for JavaScipt/Node.js
   - AWS SDK
   - Webpack

   The Webpack library is used to bundle all JS libraries into a file. For more information, I recommend that you refer to the Webpack library at https://webpack.js.org.

3. Now you can install those required libraries for our web application using the following commands:

   ```
   $ npm install aws-iot-device-sdk --save
   $ npm install aws-sdk --save
   $ npm install webpack --save
   ```

Then you should create the following files:

- `aws-configuration.js`
- `webpack.config.js`
- `entry.js`
- `index.html`

4. For data the visualization framework, we will use the Flot library. You should put the Flot library and jQuery files into the project. You can see the project structure in the following screenshot:

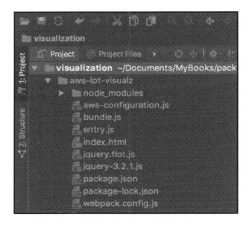

5. We start working with the `aws-configuration.js` file. This consists of AWS IoT configuration. You should fill in the `poolId` for the AWS Cognito identity pool that we have already created in the previous section:

```
var awsConfiguration = {
 poolId: '<cognito-pool-id>', // 'YourCognitoIdentityPoolId'
 host: '<aws-iot-host>.iot.<region>.amazonaws.com', //
'YourAwsIoTEndpoint', e.g. 'prefix.iot.us-east-1.amazonaws.com'
 region: '<region>' // 'YourAwsRegion', e.g. 'us-east-1'
};
module.exports = awsConfiguration;
```

6. Next, we configure our webpack in the `webpack.config.js` file. We set the `entry` value with the `entry.js` file. The result of the webpack generator is the `bundle.js` file that will be used by our HTML5 application. The following is the content of the `webpack.config.js` file:

```
module.exports = {
 entry: "./entry.js",
 output: {
 path: __dirname,
 filename: "bundle.js"
 },
 node: {
 fs: 'empty',
 tls: 'empty'
 }
};
```

`entry.js` is an application core that retrieves data from AWS IoT using AWS IoT SDK for JavaScript/Node.js.

7. Firstly, we initialize `AWS`, `AWSIoTData`, and `AWSConfiguration`. All sensor data will be stored into the `sensor_data` array. The counter will be used to indicate a number of sensor data. `clientId` is used as a browser identity:

```
var AWS = require('aws-sdk');
var AWSIoTData = require('aws-iot-device-sdk');
var AWSConfiguration = require('./aws-configuration.js');

console.log('Loaded AWS SDK for JavaScript and AWS IoT SDK for
Node.js');

var currentlySubscribedTopic = 'iot/sensor';
var clientId = 'mqtt-explorer-' + (Math.floor((Math.random() *
100000) + 1));

// sensor data
var sensor_data = [];
var counter = 0;
```

8. We load the AWS configuration from the `aws-configuration.js` file. Then, we create an instance of `device` from AWS IoT, as shown in the following code:

```
AWS.config.region = AWSConfiguration.region;
AWS.config.credentials = new AWS.CognitoIdentityCredentials({
 IdentityPoolId: AWSConfiguration.poolId
```

```
});

const mqttClient = AWSIoTData.device({
 region: AWS.config.region,
 host:AWSConfiguration.host,
 clientId: clientId,
 protocol: 'wss',
 maximumReconnectTimeMs: 8000,
 debug: true,
 accessKeyId: '',
 secretKey: '',
 sessionToken: ''
});
```

9. We also create an instance for `cognitoIdentity`. Then, we make a credential from the AWS IoT:

```
var cognitoIdentity = new AWS.CognitoIdentity();
AWS.config.credentials.get(function(err, data) {
 if (!err) {
 console.log('retrieved identity: ' +
AWS.config.credentials.identityId);
 var params = {
 IdentityId: AWS.config.credentials.identityId
 };

 ...

 } else {
 console.log('error retrieving identity:' + err);
 alert('error retrieving identity: ' + err);
 }
});
```

10. In the last step for writing the program on `entry.js`, we listen to three events from MQTT: `connect`, `reconnect`, and `message`. All the sensor data coming will raise the `message` event. When the sensor data comes, we put this data into an array of sensor `sensor_data` and then increment the `counter` value:

```
window.mqttClientConnectHandler = function() {
 console.log('connect');
 $("#status").text("Connected to AWS IoT.");

 mqttClient.subscribe(currentlySubscribedTopic);
};
```

```
window.mqttClientReconnectHandler = function() {
  console.log('reconnect');
  $("#status").text("Connected to AWS IoT.");
};
...

window.updatePublishTopic = function() {};

mqttClient.on('connect', window.mqttClientConnectHandler);
mqttClient.on('reconnect', window.mqttClientReconnectHandler);
mqttClient.on('message', window.mqttClientMessageHandler);
```

11. This is the end of writing for the `entry.js` file. Now we can continue to write a program for the `index.html` file. The web application `index.html`, will use the `bundle.js` that will be generated by the webpack. We visualize the sensor data using the Flot framework. The following is the complete program for the `index.html` file:

```
<html>
<head>
 <meta charset="UTF-8">
 <title>Sensor Visualization for AWS IoT</title>
 <script language="javascript" type="text/javascript"
src="jquery-3.2.1.js"></script>
 <script language="javascript" type="text/javascript"
src="jquery.flot.js"></script>
</head>
<body>
 <h2>Data Visualization for AWS IoT</h2>
 <span id="status"></span>
 <br>
 <div id="placeholder" style="width:600px;height:300px;"></div>
 <script src="bundle.js"></script>

</body>
</html>
```

We are done with developing the frontend application using HTML5.

12. Now we should build a webpack to generate the `bundle.js` file. Open the Terminal and navigate to the project folder. Then, type the following command:

```
$ ./node_modules/.bin/webpack --config webpack.config.js
```

This should generate the `bundle.js` file.

In the next section, we will run the project for testing.

Running the project

After we have configured and developed programs for the backend and frontend, we will compile and run the program. Consider the following steps:

1. Firstly, we run the backend application, `sensor-publisher.js`. You can open the Terminal and navigate to the sensor publisher project. Then, type the following command:

```
$ node sensor-publisher.js
```

2. After execution, we continue to run the frontend application. Run `index.html` on your web server. Then, open the browser and navigate to `http://<server>/index.html`. You should see the sensor data visualization, as shown in the following screenshot:

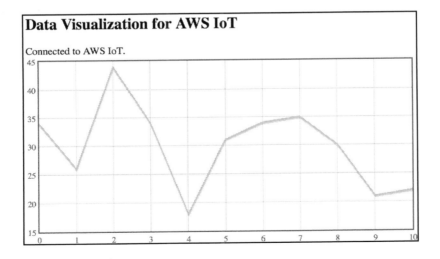

You also should see the program output on the backend app:

```
agusk$ node sensor-publisher.js
Sensor publisher started.
connected to AWS IoT.
sent:   {"temperature":34}
sent:   {"temperature":26}
sent:   {"temperature":44}
sent:   {"temperature":34}
sent:   {"temperature":18}
sent:   {"temperature":31}
sent:   {"temperature":34}
sent:   {"temperature":35}
sent:   {"temperature":30}
sent:   {"temperature":21}
sent:   {"temperature":22}
sent:   {"temperature":13}
```

Introducing Amazon QuickSight

In the previous section, we learned how to visualize sensor data from AWS IoT. We used Flot to generate data visualization. Some configurations and steps should be executed in order to visualize the data.

In this section, we will learn about Amazon QuickSight. This is one of the AWS services to visualize data for analytic purposes. Amazon QuickSight can visualize any data from any source. You should configure your data source in order to work with Amazon QuickSight.

 For further information on Amazon QuickSight, visit the official website at https://quicksight.aws.

A sample of Amazon QuickSight can be seen in the following screenshot:

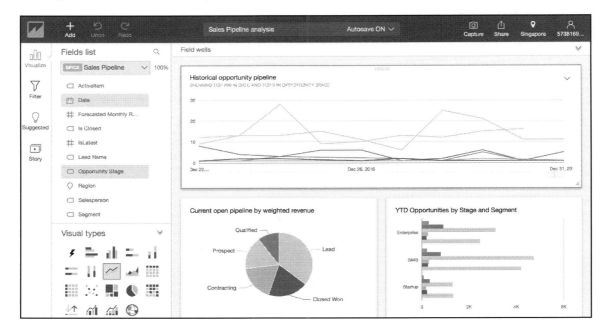

You can watch an overview of Amazon QuickSight on YouTube. Check it out at `https://www.youtube.com/watch?v=C_eT0xRNjCs`.

In general, we can upload data from CSV or Excel files to Amazon QuickSight. Then, we perform data visualization. Amazon QuickSight supports AWS data sources. The following is a list of AWS data source that works with Amazon QuickSight:

- Amazon Redshift
- Amazon RDS
- Amazon Aurora
- Amazon Athena
- Amazon S3
- Amazon EMR (Presto and Apache Spark)

If you have legacy database engines, such as SQL Server, MySQL, or PostgreSQL, you can connect them to the Amazon QuickSight.

Consuming sensor data from Amazon QuickSight

To consume sensor data from Amazon QuickSight, we should provide supported sensor data sources. For the demo, we will consume sensor data from the Excel file. I have prepared this data. You can download it from `https://github.com/agusk/awsiot/raw/master/data/Sensor-Data.xlsx`.

To implement this demo, perform the following steps:

1. The first step to implement this demo is to register with Amazon QuickSight. At the time of writing, it provides a free scheme with a limited 1 GB storage. You can register at `https://quicksight.aws`.

2. Next, we create sensor data. For this demo, I will prepare sensor data in Excel. You can download it at `https://github.com/agusk/awsiot/raw/master/data/Sensor-Data.xlsx`. You can also create your own sensor data. In general, this sensor data consists of temperature and humidity, as shown in the following screenshot. This data will be uploaded to Amazon QuickSight:

No	Temperature	Humidity
1	11	65
2	28	67
3	24	35
4	29	58
5	10	39
6	25	79
7	23	39
8	15	72
9	29	43
10	16	62
11	16	76
12	26	68
13	17	73
14	13	57
15	11	51
16	22	73
17	24	75
18	15	51
19	29	71
20	11	43
21	18	34
22	19	74
23	27	77
24	11	39
25	11	33
26	14	51
27	26	33
28	26	65
29	28	31
30	22	46

3. Open Amazon QuickSight and select **Manage Data**. Then, you can create a new dataset by clicking on the **New data set** button.

4. Select the **Upload a file** option for the dataset type. You should get a dialog to select a file. Please select the Excel file that we have prepared. After uploading, Amazon QuickSight will detect a data sheet. Select it and then click on the **Select** button:

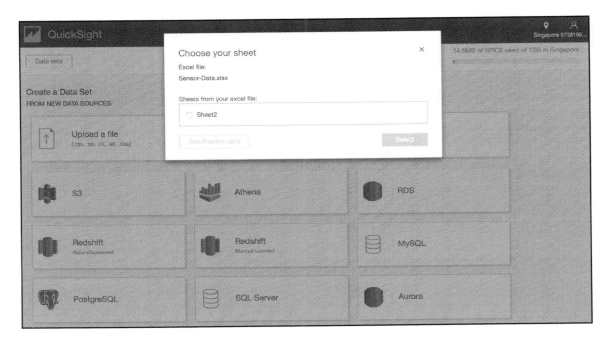

5. After selecting the data source sheet, Amazon QuickSight will display all the data. You also can edit from your uploaded data. You can see it in the following screenshot:

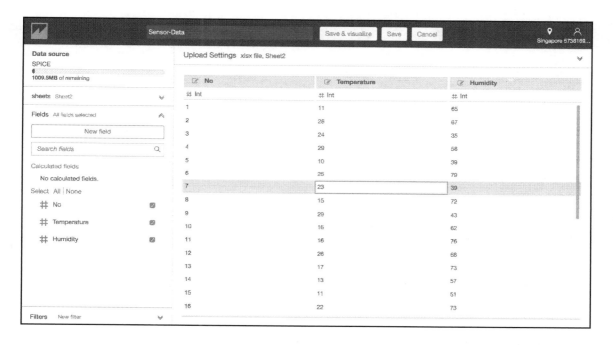

6. Next, we can visualize this data directly. Click on the **Save & visualize** button to perform data visualization. We can create a simple chart. You can select the Line chart from the **Visual types** section. Then, select No for the **X axis** field. For the **Value** field, you can select Temperature and Humidity. A result of the data visualization can be seen in the following screenshot:

7. You can create other visual models by selecting them in the **Visual types** section. For instance, I selected a stacked bar combo chart type. Then, select `No` for the **X axis**, `Temperature` for **Bars,** and `Humidity` for **Lines**. You can see the result of the data visualization in the following screenshot:

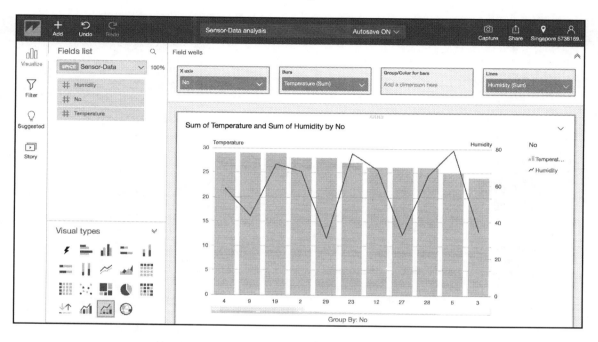

What's next? You can modify and do experimentation for this data visualization. You can change the visual type and select data sources on the chart.

Building data visualization for your IoT projects

We have learned how to visualize sensor data using the JavaScript library. The data can come from the IoT device directly or probably be consumed from Amazon AWS. In the context of data streaming to serve huge IoT device requests, we can use AWS IoT as the frontend from the cloud system to address huge requests. Since Amazon AWS is built from cloud technology, we are confident about its availability.

In general, we can build an IoT project by combining various AWS services, as shown in the following figure:

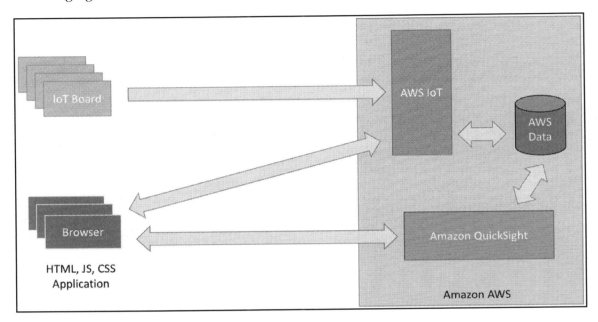

You select the IoT device that should be supported by AWS IoT. If not supported, you should build your own library that enables accessing AWS IoT. Within AWS IoT, you can save in the local AWS using various AWS services, such as Amazon RDS, Amazon EC2 with the installed SQL Server, MySQL, or PostgreSQL.

We have learned to visualize sensor data directly from AWS IoT with the publisher/subscriber. You can implement data visualization with your own scenario. Alternatively, we can use Amazon QuickSight. Your data should be stored on datasets that are supported by Amazon QuickSight.

Summary

We have now learned how to work with data visualization. We have implemented data visualization with various JavaScript engines. We have also performed data visualization from AWS IoT. Finally, we explored Amazon QuickSight and performed data visualization.

In the next chapter, we will learn how to build predictive analytics with AWS IoT and AWS Machine Learning.

7

Building Predictive Analytics for AWS IoT

Machine learning is one of the potential technologies that has multiple benefits when applied to our business cases. In this chapter, you will learn various Amazon AWS services related to machine learning. Some demos will be explored using machine learning services from Amazon.

The following is a list of topics covered in this chapter:

- Introducing AWS Machine Learning services
- Making your sensor speak
- Integrating Amazon Echo into your IoT projects
- Making image and video analysis
- Making predictive analytics for IoT data

Introducing AWS Machine Learning services

Machine learning is one of the subjects in computer science that describes how to teach computers to obtain the ability to learn without hardcoding in a program. More specifically, machine learning enables computers to learn from experiences such as data, information, and training results from experts.

All AWS Machine Learning services can be found at `https://aws.amazon.com/machine-learning/`. At the time of writing this book, AWS Machine Learning services are available in any region. Make sure that you change AWS region in order to enable AWS Machine Learning services:

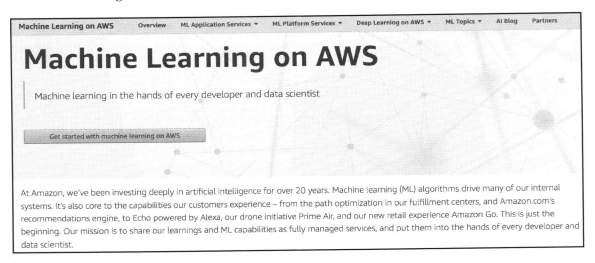

In this chapter, we will explore some AWS Machine Learning services that are related to IoT topics.

Making your sensor speak

Suppose that you have deployed sensors at various locations. Those sensors perform monitoring to detect a specific purpose. When a sensor finds a thing that its looking for, a sensor device will send an alert to a command center. Some people probably stand by on that location. When an alert comes, the system can make a sound through a speaker.

Message-to-sound or text-to-speech is a field of speech technology that leverages machine learning. A system can convert text or message to human speech. In general, the scenario can be described in the following figure:

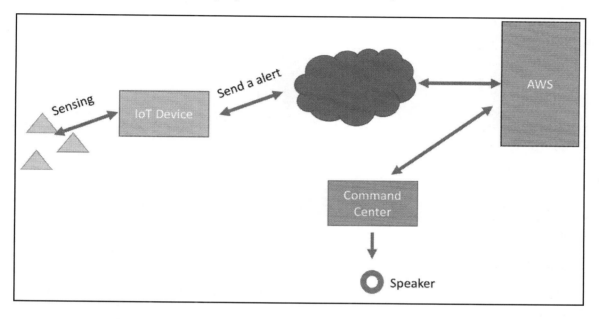

From the preceding figure, IoT device can perform sensing and send data to AWS. IoT device can send an alert message to AWS to inform to the command center. AWS can convert text message to sound message. Once a command center receives a sound message, it performs to generate sound through a speaker.

Amazon AWS provides a service that applies speech technology, named **Amazon Polly**. You will learn how to work with Amazon Polly and then access it from a program in the next sections.

Introducing Amazon Polly

Amazon Polly is one of the AWS services that enables your application such as IoT program to talk using lifelike speech. You can find this service at `https://aws.amazon.com/polly/`. You can see it in the following screenshot:

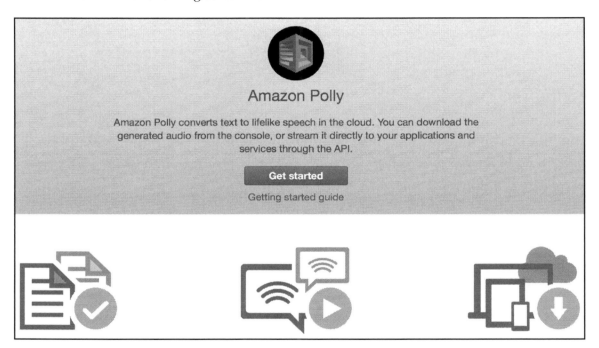

If you have an active Amazon account, you can access Amazon Polly at `http://console.aws.amazon.com/polly/` through a browser. Currently, Amazon Polly provides two features—**Text-to-Speech** and **Lexicons**. You can test these features on the browser.

In order to test the **Text-to-Speech** feature, click on the **Plain text** tab and fill a text or message. Then, select the **Voice** model that you prefer. Once done, click on the **Listen to speech** button to listen to speech from the text/message:

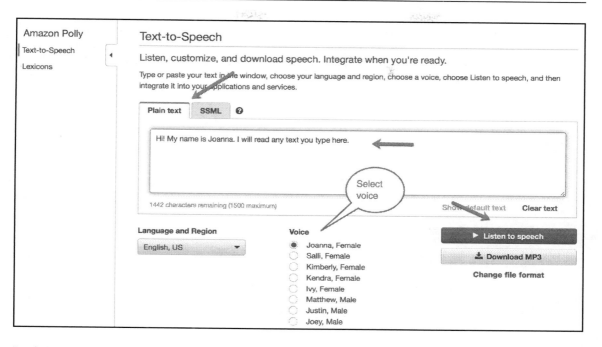

In the next section, we will develop a program to access AWS Polly from Node.js.

Developing a program for Amazon Polly

In the previous section, we have access to the text-to-speech feature from Amazon Polly. In this section, we try to access it from a program. This is useful when you apply Polly on IoT devices such as Raspberry Pi:

1. To access Amazon Polly, we need to prepare the account with privilege access for AWS Polly. First, you can access the AWS IAM dashboard on `http://console.aws.amazon.com/iam/`. Then, create a new user if you don't have it yet.

2. Now you can configure your user to give permission to access Amazon Polly. Open your IAM user that is shown in the following screenshot. Then, click on the **Add permissions** button. Find **AmazonPollyFullAccess** policy and add it into your IAM user:

3. Next, you should copy the AWS access key ID from your IAM user. You can find it under the **Security credentials** tab. You can create an AWS access key if you don't have it. This AWS access key ID will be used in our program.

4. For testing, we use Node.js to develop a program. We need AWS SDK for JavaScript/Node.js to access Amazon Polly. This program can run on Raspberry Pi 3 and on computer. You can type the following commands for creating a project and installing AWS SDK for JavaScript/Node.js:

```
$ mkdir ml
$ cd ml/
$ npm init
$ npm install aws-sdk --save
```

5. We will use the `Polly` object to access AWS Polly from Node.js. You can read more information about the `Polly` object on `https://docs.aws.amazon.com/AWSJavaScriptSDK/latest/AWS/Polly.html`. We pass our AWS access key ID to perform AWS authentication.

6. To convert from text-to-speech, we can call `Polly.synthesizeSpeech()`. From this process, we can save the result into an MP3 file.

7. Let's create a file, `aws-polly-demo.js`. Then, write code snippet. Change `<accessKeyId>` by your AWS access key ID that you have copied:

```
const AWS = require('aws-sdk')
const Fs = require('fs')

var accessKeyId = '<accessKeyId>';
const Polly = new AWS.Polly({
 accessKeyId: accessKeyId,
 signatureVersion: 'v4',
 region: 'us-east-1'
});

...
Polly.synthesizeSpeech(params, (err, data) => {
 if (err) {
    console.log(err);
 } else if (data) {
   if (data.AudioStream instanceof Buffer) {
     Fs.writeFile("./temperature.mp3", data.AudioStream,
function(err) {
        if (err) {
          return console.log(err)
        }
        console.log("temperature.mp3 file was saved!")
     })
   }
 }
});
```

8. Save this program and run it using the following command:

```
$ node aws-polly-demo.js
```

9. You should see the MP3 file from the executing result. You can see the program output that is shown in the following screenshot. Try to run that MP3 file:

```
agusk$ node aws-polly-demo.js
temperature.mp3 file was saved!
agusk$
```

Sometimes, you want this program to play the MP3 file directly or you want to execute text-to-speech to speaker directly through streaming MP3.

10. To work with the speaker on the local computer or Raspberry Pi 3, we can use node-speaker library. Further information about node-speaker, I recommend to read it on `https://github.com/TooTallNate/node-speaker`. You can install this library by typing this command:

```
$ npm install speaker
```

11. If you are working on macOS, you will probably get errors. You can run this command to solve the error on macOS:

```
$ XX=clang++ npm install speaker --mpg123-backend=openal
```

You can read *node-speaker* document on Github if you still get errors while running this library.

12. Now we modify our previous program to play text-to-speech streaming into node-speaker library. Create the `sensor-speaker.js` file and write this code snippet:

```
const AWS = require('aws-sdk')
const Stream = require('stream')
const Speaker = require('speaker')

...
Polly.synthesizeSpeech(params, (err, data) => {
 if (err) {
   console.log(err);
 } else if (data) {
   if (data.AudioStream instanceof Buffer) {

     var bufferStream = new Stream.PassThrough();
     bufferStream.end(data.AudioStream);
     bufferStream.pipe(Player);

   }else{
     console.log('data is not AudioStream');
   }
 }
});
```

This program will put `AudioStream` from AWS Polly into the `Stream` object. Then, we play by calling the `pipe()` function.

13. Now you can run this program by typing the following command:

```
$ node sensor-speaker.js
```

You should listen sound from the speaker. Make sure that your speaker is already attached to Raspberry Pi 3 or local computer.

What's next? You can modify this program based on your case. You can add an alert-based speech into your other IoT projects.

Integrating Amazon Echo into your IoT projects

Amazon Echo is one of the Amazon products that uses speech technology. Amazon developed **Artificial Intelligence (AI)** to enable interaction with machines through speech. You can buy Amazon Echo on the Amazon website at `https://www.amazon.com/dp/B06XCM9LJ4/`. Unfortunately, Amazon Echo probably does not support for your country. A list of supported countries includes their features can be found on this website `https://www.amazon.com/gp/help/customer/display.html?nodeId=202207000`.

Amazon also provides a lite version from Amazon Echo known as **Amazon Echo Dot**. You can buy it on `https://www.amazon.com/gp/product/B01DFKC2SO/`. I bought this device from Amazon Germany. You can see my Amazon Echo Dot in the following image:

In this section, we will build a project to integrate between Amazon Echo and IoT board. In general, we develop a program based on a scenario in the following figure. We want to turn on/off the LED by giving a voice command. For instance, I would say **Alexa ask Zahra turn on LED**. **Alexa** and **Zahra** are predefined keywords. **Alexa** is a keyword from Amazon Echo to give a command. **Zahra** is my own keyword that is built from Amazon to call my program. The **turn on LED** or **turn off LED** is one of the commands that I have prepared. This command will perform to turn on/off an LED that is attached on Raspberry Pi 3 or other IoT board:

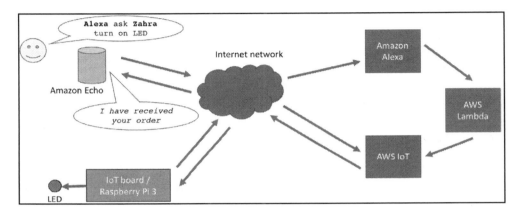

How does the project work? From the preceding figure, we send specific words to Amazon Echo. This speech command will be sent to Amazon Alexa. Since we involve IoT stuffs in this project, we should connect AWS Lambda and AWS IoT into Amazon Alexa.

We can attach an LED into the board. We make a program to communicate with AWS IoT. Once AWS IoT receives a message from Amazon Alexa through AWS Lambda, IoT board will perform a task based on the incoming command.

It is our demo scenario. Next, we will build the project by performing a number of tasks as follows:

1. Preparing a project
2. Adding user role on Amazon IAM
3. Configuring AWS IoT
4. Creating AWS Lambda
5. Building Amazon Alexa skill
6. Testing project

We will perform each task in the next section.

Preparing the project

To implement this project, you should have Amazon Echo or Amazon Echo Dot. You can buy this device on the Amazon website. Fortunately, we can use the speech simulator from Amazon Alexa to emulate Amazon Echo. We send a voice command to test the program.

In addition, you should have an active account for the AWS and Amazon Alexa developer. In *Chapter 1*, *Getting Started with AWS IoT*, you probably registered to Amazon AWS. We will explore the Amazon Alexa developer in the next section of this chapter.

Adding user role

Because Amazon Alexa calls AWS Lambda and AWS Lambda calls AWS IoT, we need a role to cover an access right for Amazon Alexa and AWS IoT. You can add a new role on Amazon IAM at `http://console.aws.amazon.com/iam/`. For instance, I created a role, named `alexarole`. Then, we should attach policies related to Amazon Alexa and AWS IoT. You probably can add **AWSIoTDataAccess** and **AlexaForBusinessFullAccess**. You can see my account role in AWS IoT that is shown in the following screenshot:

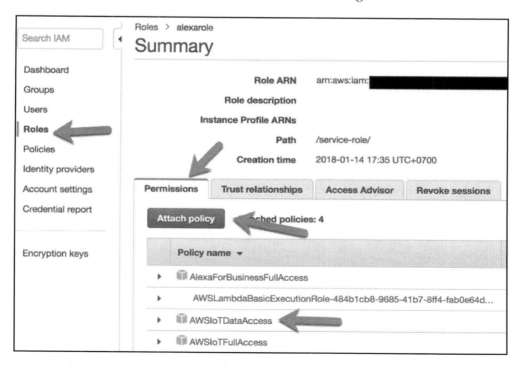

Configuring AWS IoT

The next step is to configure AWS IoT. If you have performed each demo from chapters 1 to 6, you should have enough experience to work with AWS IoT.

In this demo, you should register one device that will be used for making interactions with AWS IoT. You also need to note your AWS IoT hostname. It will be used on Amazon Alexa.

Creating AWS Lambda

After creating a role from AWS IAM, we should create AWS Lambda. We can create AWS Lambda with the template from Blueprints:

1. You can find **alexa-skills-kit-color-expert** by filtering with the `alexa` keyword, as shown in the following screenshot:

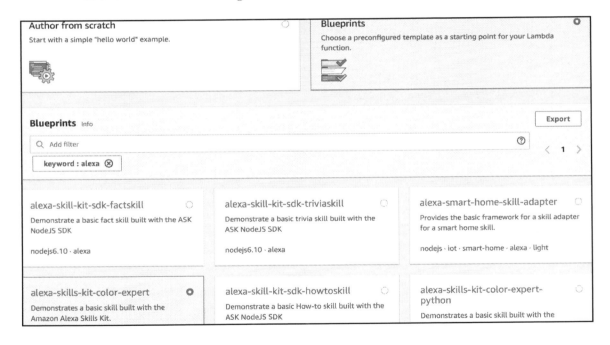

2. You can create AWS Lambda from the **alexa-skills-kit-color-expert** template. Then, fill your Lambda function name, for instance, `fxalexa`. Select a role from the existing roles that you have already created. Otherwise, you can create a new role and then configure it to give permission to access AWS IoT and Amazon Alexa, as shown in the following screenshot:

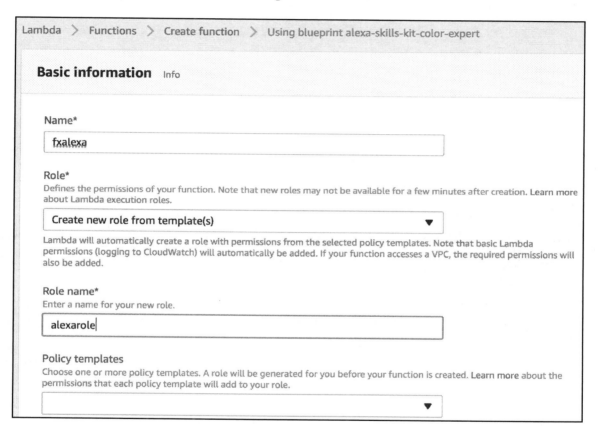

3. You should see a Lambda editor that is shown in the following screenshot. You should also see Lambda ARN. We will use it for Amazon Alexa:

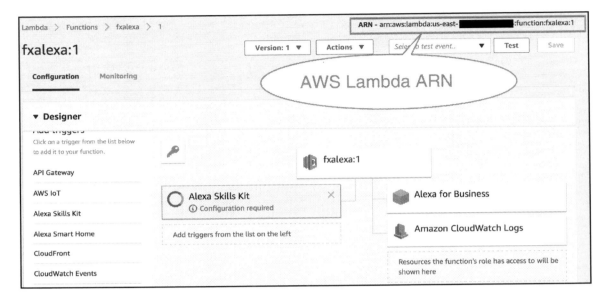

4. Now we will modify the program on the `index.js` file to make a Lambda communicate with Amazon Alexa and AWS IoT.

5. On the top of the `index.js` file, we add scripts. We access AWS IoT through AWS SDK for JavaScript. You should set the AWS IoT region and hostname that you have noted from the previous section:

```
var AWS = require('aws-sdk');
var iotdata = new AWS.IotData({region: '<region>', endpoint:
'<hostname>.iot.<region>.amazonaws.com'});
```

6. Next, we modify the `onIntent()` function. We add script to filter SmartLED from the Alexa intent name. If we have `SmartLED` intent name, we call the `performLEDInSession()` function. All scripts should be remarked since we don't use those. The following is a complete script for the `onIntent()` function:

```
function onIntent(intentRequest, session, callback) {
    console.log(`onIntent requestId=${intentRequest.requestId},
sessionId=${session.sessionId}`);

    const intent = intentRequest.intent;
    const intentName = intentRequest.intent.name;
```

```
// Dispatch to your skill's intent handlers
if (intentName === 'SmartLED') {
    performLEDInSession(intent, session, callback);

} else if (intentName === 'AMAZON.StopIntent' || intentName
=== 'AMAZON.CancelIntent') {
    handleSessionEndRequest(callback);
} else {
    throw new Error('Invalid intent');
}
}
```

7. Then, we can define the `performLEDInSession()` function. This function will check an Alexa command value. If the Alexa command is valid, we will pass it to AWS IoT. We send a message on AWS IoT message topic `alexa/led`. The Alexa command value will be set on the payload of the AWS IoT message. You can call the `publish()` function to send the message to AWS IoT:

```
function performLEDInSession(intent, session, callback) {
    const cardTitle = intent.name;
    const actionSlot = intent.slots.LEDState;
    let repromptText = '';
    let sessionAttributes = {};
    const shouldEndSession = false;
    let speechOutput = '';

    ...

        iotdata.publish(params, function(err, data){
            if(err){
                console.log(err);
            }
            else{
                console.log(data);
                console.log("sending to IoT message was success");
            }
        });

    } else {
        speechOutput = "I'm not sure what your order. Please try
again.";
        repromptText = "I'm not sure what your order. Please try
again.";
    }

    callback(sessionAttributes, buildSpeechletResponse(cardTitle,
speechOutput, repromptText, shouldEndSession));
}
```

From the preceding code, we can see the `speechOutput` variable. It will be sent back to Amazon Echo. Then, those words will be sounded by Amazon Echo. If the Alexa command is valid, Amazon Echo will say `I have received your order`. Otherwise, it will say `I'm not sure what your order is. Please try again.`

Now you are done creating AWS Lambda. You can save and then publish this AWS Lambda. Next, we will develop Amazon Alexa skills, so Amazon Echo can detect our speech command.

Building Amazon Alexa skills

Amazon Echo consists of speech commands that come from the official Amazon and third parties. Amazon requires an Amazon developer account to develop programs on top of Amazon Echo. You should register Amazon Alexa developer through the website on `https://developer.amazon.com/alexa`.

In this section, we will develop a new skill for Amazon Echo. We want our Amazon Echo to detect our voice command to turn on/off LED. After registration on Amazon Alexa developer, you visit developer console. Click on the **ALEXA** tab. You should get two options that are shown in the following screenshot:

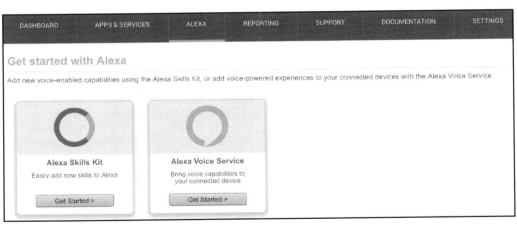

Proceed with the steps as follows:

1. To create a new Alexa skill, you can click on the **Alexa Skills Kit** section. You should see a list of Alexa skills that you have created. You can see this list in the following screenshot:

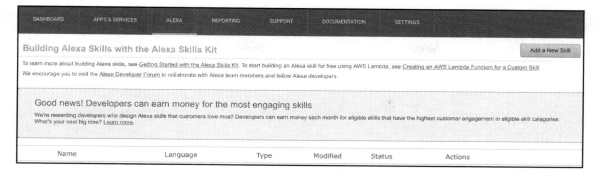

2. Next, you can click on the **Add a New Skill** button to create a new Alexa skill. Then, you will get a screen that is shown in the following screenshot.

3. Select language, for instance, **English (U.S.)**. You are also required to fill in a skill name and invocation name. The **Invocation Name** field is used for Alexa to call our program. In this program, I fill in `Zahra`. It means that the program will be called by sending the speech command `Alexa ask Zahra ...`:

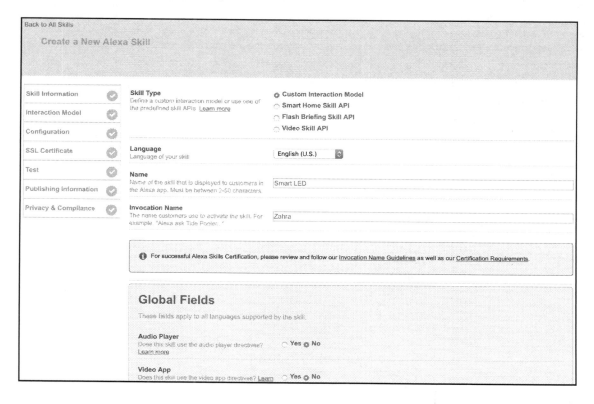

Once all the fields are filled, click on the **Next** button.

4. Now you will get the **Interaction Model** section that is shown in the following screenshot. In this screen, we build speech commands for our demo:

5. First, we build intent schema with the name SmartLED. You can write these scripts in the **Intent Schema** field:

```
{
  "intents": [
      {
        "slots": [
            {
              "name": "LEDState",
              "type": "LED_STATE"
            }
          ],
        "intent": "SmartLED"
      }
```

```
                ]
            }
```

6. You can see that we declare slots with the name `LEDState`. We need to define these slots in the **Custom Slot Types** section. Fill `LED_STATE` in the **Enter Type** field. You also fill `on` and `off` in the **Enter Values** section .

7. You should also fill the following scripts for `utterances`. For that, please write these scripts:

```
SmartLED Turn {LEDState} LED
SmartLED Turn LED {LEDState}
```

Once you have completed the building interaction model, you can click on the **Next** button.

8. Now you have the **Configuration** screen that is shown in the following screenshot. For demo, we set **AWS Lambda ARN (Amazon Resource Name)** for endpoint. You put AWS Lambda ARN in the **Default** field from your note on the previous section:

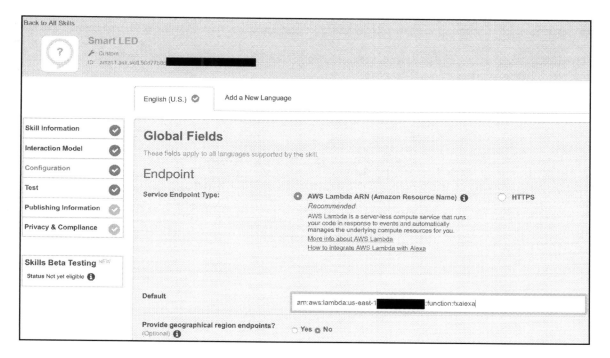

Once done, you can click on the **Next** button.

9. From this task, we can continue to **publish** to **public** by following instruction from Alexa skill. For demo, I didn't publish it, so this program only runs on my own Amazon Echo. You can verify your Amazon Alexa on Android or iOS. Then, your Alexa skill shows on that program. You can see my Alexa skills on iOS program that is shown in the following screenshot:

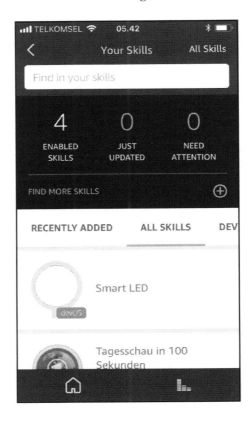

Now your project is ready for testing. We will perform this task on the next section.

Testing the project

For testing, we can use the **Service Simulator** section from the Amazon Alexa. You can find it on the **Test** menu from your Alexa skill. Follow the steps as follows:

1. Fill `turn on LED` in the **Enter Utterance** field. You can see it in the following screenshot. Click on a button, for my case, it shows the **Ask Smart LED** button.

2. After execution, the program will send a JSON message to AWS Lambda. Then, you should get a response from AWS Lambda. A sample of the response from AWS Lambda can be seen in the following screenshot:

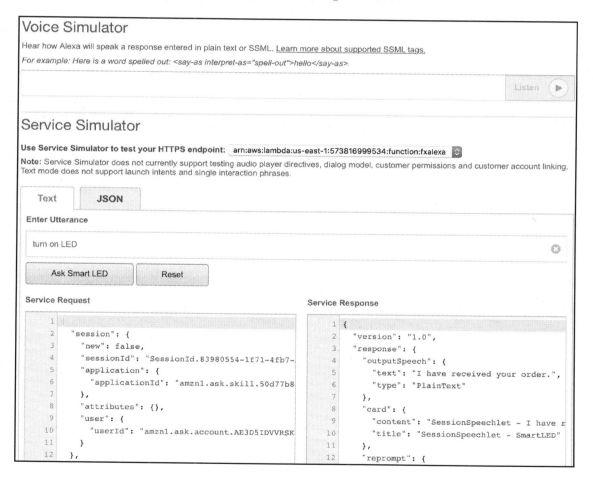

If you have a response with outputSpeech `I have received your order`, it means that our program works.

3. Now you open AWS IoT and run the **Test** program. Set `alexa/led` for subscribing a topic. Then, try to execute Service Simulator from Amazon Alexa. You should get a response with message on. You can also try to send the message `turn off LED` on the Service Simulator:

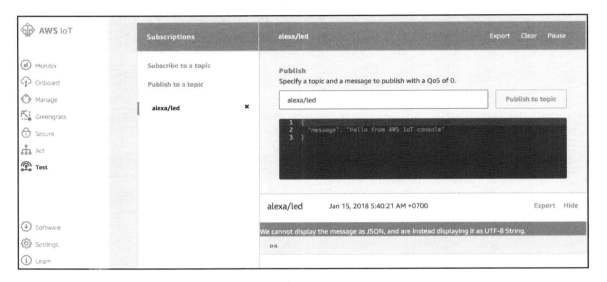

4. Now we can make a program to subscribe `alexa/led` on IoT board such as Raspberry Pi. When we receive the `on` message from the AWS IoT, we can perform to turn on LED. Otherwise, we can perform to turn off LED when we receive the `off` message.

5. For demo, I created a program to subscribe `alexa/led`. Once message is received, the program will print it on the console. Create the `alexa-demo.js` file and write this complete program for this demo:

```
var awsIot = require('aws-iot-device-sdk');

var device = awsIot.device({
    keyPath: '<device>-private.pem.key',
    certPath: '<device>-certificate.pem.crt',
    caPath: 'cert/root-CA.pem',
    host: '<iot-host>.iot.<region>.amazonaws.com',
    clientId: 'user-testing',
    region: '<region>'
```

```
    });

device
    .on('connect', function() {
      console.log('connected');
      device.subscribe('alexa/led');
    });

device
  .on('message', function(topic, payload) {
      var order = payload.toString();
      if(order=='on'){
         console.log('turn on LED');
         // perform turn on LED
         //
      }else{
         console.log('turn off LED');
         // perform turn off LED
         //
      }
    });

      console.log('AWS IoT - Alexa program started.');
```

This program is modified from Chapter 2, *Connecting IoT Devices to the AWS IoT Platform*. Once done, save this program and run it by typing the following command:

```
$ node alexa-demo.js
```

6. You can test again to send speech commands from the **Service Simulator** section on Amazon Alexa. This program will receive that command. You can see a sample of program output in the following screenshot:

```
agusk$ node alexa-demo.js
AWS IoT - Alexa program started.
connected
turn on LED
turn off LED
```

Finally, you have learned how to work with Amazon Echo and AWS IoT and make interaction. Next, you can learn about *Alexa Skills Kit* from the official document on https:/ /developer.amazon.com/docs/ask-overviews/build-skills-with-the-alexa-skills- kit.html.

Making image and video analysis

In this section, we learn how to analyze image and video. Machine learning can perform pattern recognition for a picture or a video. The result of machine learning analysis can be object detection or image analysis.

For instance, I have a still image; this image is analyzed using machine learning. It shows some identified objects, such as human, brick, clothing, and coat. You can see it in the following image. This process is done using **Amazon Rekognition**:

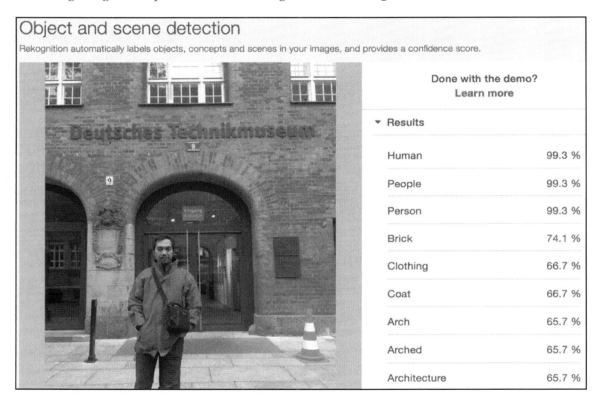

In this section, we focus on how to use Amazon Rekognition to analyze image and video. Setting and configuring will be performed in the next section.

Introducing Amazon Rekognition

Amazon Rekognition is one of the Amazon services that is part of Amazon Machine Learning. You just register and activate your AWS account on this services. Amazon Rekognition can perform object and scene detection, image moderation, facial analysis, celebrity recognition, face comparison, text in image analysis, and video analysis. Technically, Amazon Rekognition applies deep learning algorithms for machine learning implementation.

You can visit Amazon Rekognition console on `https://console.aws.amazon.com/rekognition/`. Try to see some demos for this service, as shown in the following screenshot. Some demo scenarios are shown in the left-hand menu. Just click on the **Demos** menu and select a picture; you will see a result of image analysis on the right side. You also can upload your own image file and try to analyze it:

For demo in this section, we will develop to perform image analysis. We will detect objects in an image using Amazon Rekognition. In general, our demo can be described in the following figure:

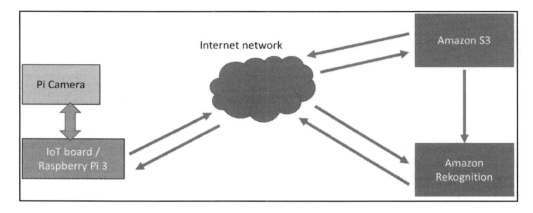

From the preceding figure, a camera is attached on Raspberry Pi. We develop a program to upload a picture file to Amazon S3. Then, we analyze the image file from Amazon S3 using Amazon Rekognition.

Next, we configure Pi Camera on Raspberry Pi in next section.

Working with Pi Camera on Raspberry Pi

Raspberry Pi Foundation provides an official cameras for Raspberry Pi. A list of Raspberry Pi cameras can be found at https://www.raspberrypi.org/documentation/hardware/camera/README.md. I have two official camera modules from Raspberry Pi. They are **Pi Camera v2** and **Pi NoIR Camera v2**. You can see them in the following image:

To work with Pi Camera, I recommend to read the official document on this site at `https://www.raspberrypi.org/documentation/raspbian/applications/camera.md`. You also can learn Pi Camera on this site, `https://projects.raspberrypi.org/en/projects/getting-started-with-picamera/`. After taking a picture using Pi Camera, you can start to write a program to upload to Amazon S3.

Another solution for Pi Camera is that you can use any camera USB that is attached through USB from Raspberry Pi. Make sure that you can access it and click a picture.

We will upload a picture file to Amazon S3 in the next section.

Uploading images to Amazon S3

Amazon S3 is one of the Amazon services that stores files, content, and blob. You can manage Amazon S3 on `https://s3.console.aws.amazon.com/`. In this section, we will upload the following image with the name `IMG_2222.JPG`. This file will be used to perform object detection using Amazon Rekognition:

Proceed with the steps as follows:

1. First, we should create a bucket on Amazon S3. All the image files will be uploaded to this bucket. You can navigate to `https://s3.console.aws.amazon.com/` on the browser. Click on the **+ Create bucket** button and follow the steps to create a bucket on Amazon S3. For instance, I created a bucket named `akurs3` that is shown in the following screenshot:

2. Next, we develop a program to upload a picture file to Amazon S3.

3. For demo, we developed a program using Node.js. We can use AWS SDK for JavaScript/Node.js. We use the S3 object from the AWS SDK. To upload a file, we can call the upload() function with passing the file and bucket name. You need accessKeyId to access Amazon S3. You can get it from the Amazon IAM. You have learned it from Chapter 6, *Visualizing Your AWS IoT Data*.

4. Create the upload-s3.js file and write the following complete script:

```
var AWS = require('aws-sdk');
var fs = require('fs');

console.log('Demo uploading a file to Amazon S3.');
var accessKeyId = '<accessKeyId>';
const s3bucket = new AWS.S3({
    accessKeyId: accessKeyId,
    signatureVersion: 'v4',
    region: 'us-east-1'
});

var filepath ='./IMG_2222.JPG';
var filename = 'IMG_2222.JPG';
console.log('Uploading ',filename, ' to Amazon S3.');
console.log(filename);
var params = {
    Key: filename,
    Body: fs.createReadStream(filepath),
    Bucket: '<s3-bucket>'
};
console.log('uploading...');
s3bucket.upload(params, function (err, res) {
    if(err)
```

```
                    console.log("Error in uploading file on s3. Error: "+
           err)
              else
                    console.log("File successfully uploaded.")
           });
```

5. You can change `filename` for your testing image file and `filepath` for path of image file.

6. Save this program and execute it using this command:

   $ node upload-s3.js

On successful execution, you can see verbose messages on the Terminal, as shown in the following screenshot:

```
agusk$ node upload-s3.js
Demo uploading a file to Amazon S3.
Uploading  IMG_2222.JPG  to Amazon S3.
IMG_2222.JPG
uploading...
File successfully uploaded.
agusk$
```

After uploading the image file into the Amazon S3, we can perform image analysis using Amazon Rekognition. We do that task in the next section.

Performing image analysis

Amazon Rekognition can analyze image files from Amazon S3. You need to upload all the images in order to be analyzed by Amazon Rekognition.

In this section, we develop a program to analyze an image file. First, we should configure our account to perform image analysis using Amazon Rekognition. We can do it using Amazon IAM, as follows:

1. Open your account and add the `AmazonRekognitionXXXX` policy. For instance, I added the **AmazonRekognitionFullAccess** policy that is shown in the following screenshot:

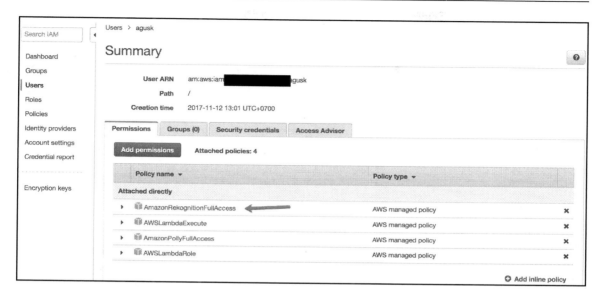

2. We create a program by creating a file named `object-rekognition.js`. To access Amazon Rekognition, we can use the `Rekognition` object from the AWS SDK. For demo, we develop a program using Node.js. You should pass `accessKeyId` and `region` from Amazon S3 into the `Rekognition` object. Amazon Rekognition will download a file from Amazon S3. Then, we can analyze the image for object detection using the `detectLabels()` function.

Now you can write this complete program for `object-rekognition.js`, as follows:

```javascript
var AWS = require('aws-sdk');
var fs = require('fs');

console.log('Demo AWS Rekognition.');
var accessKeyId = '<accessKeyId>';
const rekognition = new AWS.Rekognition({
    accessKeyId: accessKeyId,
    signatureVersion: 'v4',
    region: 'ap-northeast-1'
});

var params = {
        Image: {
            S3Object: {
                Bucket: 'akurs3',
                Name: 'IMG_2222.JPG'
```

```
                }
              }
            };
        console.log('Analyzing...');
        rekognition.detectLabels(params, function (err, data) {
            if(err)
                console.log("Error in performing AWS Rekognition. Error:
        "+ err)
            else{
                console.log("Performing AWS Rekognition is success.");
                console.log('Result:');
                console.log(data);
            }
        });
```

3. Save this program and execute it by typing this command:

```
$ node object-rekognition.js
```

You can see the result of image analysis from the Amazon Rekognition in the following screenshot. From the image file, IMG_2222.JPG, we can see a list of detected objects with the confidence degree as follows:

```
agusk$ node object-rekognition.js
Demo AWS Rekognition.
Analyzing...
Performing AWS Rekognition is success.
Result:
{ Labels:
   [ { Name: 'Electronics', Confidence: 97.94730377197266 },
     { Name: 'Monitor', Confidence: 97.94730377197266 },
     { Name: 'Screen', Confidence: 97.94730377197266 },
     { Name: 'TV', Confidence: 97.94730377197266 },
     { Name: 'Television', Confidence: 97.94730377197266 },
     { Name: 'Apartment', Confidence: 79.5370101928711 },
     { Name: 'Building', Confidence: 79.5370101928711 },
     { Name: 'Housing', Confidence: 79.5370101928711 },
     { Name: 'Indoors', Confidence: 79.5370101928711 },
     { Name: 'Room', Confidence: 64.24443054199219 },
     { Name: 'Chair', Confidence: 61.131507873535156 },
     { Name: 'Furniture', Confidence: 61.131507873535156 },
     { Name: 'Hostel', Confidence: 53.38637161254883 },
     { Name: 'Bedroom', Confidence: 52.97583770751953 },
     { Name: 'Interior Design', Confidence: 52.97583770751953 },
     { Name: 'Couch', Confidence: 51.81147003173828 },
     { Name: 'Living Room', Confidence: 51.68221664428711 },
     { Name: 'Entertainment Center', Confidence: 50.694297790527344 },
     { Name: 'Basement', Confidence: 50.66577911376953 } ] }
agusk$
```

You have learned Amazon Rekognition from the Amazon Machine Learning services. Next, you will learn to make predictive analytics for the IoT data.

Make predictive analytics for IoT data

Predictive analytics is a method to make prediction for an unknown event. In the context of IoT, we can develop predictive analytics to make a decision-based streaming sensor data. This is a part of machine learning study. In general, we can make predictive analytics using a diagram that is shown as follows:

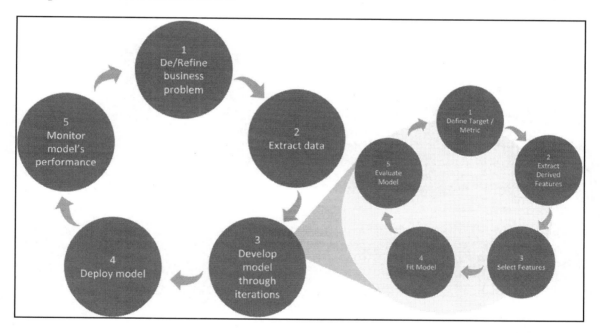

Defining business problems is the first step to develop predictive analytics. Some problems probably need experts to make clear those problems. For instance, economics, biology, and volcanology.

We also should prepare data in order to develop a model. This data should have high impact factors on the model. When we develop a model, we also perform some steps such as defining targets, extracting derived features from data, fitting the model, and evaluating the model. In a real project, we probably make some iterations to ensure the corrected model.

After we developed the model, we can deploy the model into our system. This could be deployed in web application, RESTful app, or an other platform. We also monitor how the model runs. If we find some errors in the implementation, we can modify our model and data. Then, we perform normal iteration for developing a model.

To implement a machine learning model and then evaluate the model, we can use Amazon Machine Learning. You can access it using your existing AWS account on `https://console.aws.amazon.com/machinelearning`.

Next, we will develop predictive analytics for an IoT project case using Amazon Machine Learning.

Build a simple predictive analytics for your IoT project

In this section, we will develop a simple predictive analytics for IoT. Our project can be described in the following figure. We will perform sensing to acquire temperature and humidity from the sensor devices. Then, we send this sensor data to AWS Machine Learning to get a decision on whether the system will perform watering:

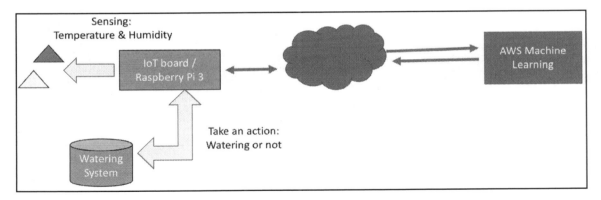

The project will focus on developing a machine learning model. Assume that we have temperature and humidity data from the sensor. We do not implement watering system, but we will make a decision system to trigger watering.

Next, we will implement the project with the following steps which are explained in detail in the upcoming sub-sections:

1. Defining a machine learning model
2. Preparing data
3. Building a machine learning model
4. Evaluating and testing a model

Defining a machine learning model

We will create a simple model for our project. We have two inputs—temperature and humidity. We also have historical data about sensor data and its decision. The system will learn from the data. You can see our project model, as shown in the following figure:

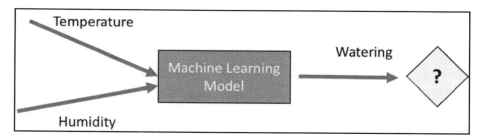

The output of model is an action—performing watering or not. This means that we perform classification computation to decide to perform watering or not.

Preparing data

After we determined a machine learning model, we can prepare the data. In this project, I generated random values for temperature and humidity. You can see this data in the following graph:

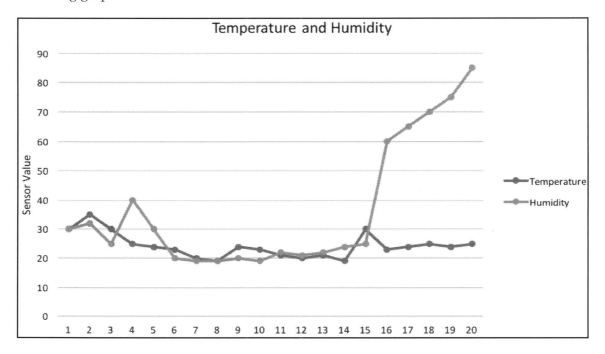

We should make the data in a CSV file. We build three columns—**Temperature**, **Humidity**, and **watering**. You can see these data in the following screenshot. The **watering** column is used for the target decision for each row's data:

Temperature	Humidity	Watering
30	30	WATERING
35	32	WATERING
30	25	WATERING
25	40	WATERING
24	30	WATERING
23	20	WATERING
20	19	WATERING
19	19	WATERING
24	20	WATERING
23	19	WATERING
21	22	NOTWATERING
20	21	NOTWATERING
21	22	NOTWATERING
19	24	NOTWATERING
30	25	NOTWATERING
23	60	NOTWATERING
24	65	NOTWATERING
25	70	NOTWATERING
24	75	NOTWATERING
25	85	NOTWATERING

Save the data into the CSV file, for instance, `Temp-Hum-Water.csv`.

We also need to create a data schema. You should create a schema file in `<data-file_name>.schema`. For our case, we create a file, `Temp-Hum-Water.csv.schema`. You can write these scripts for our schema:

```
{
"version": "1.0",
"targetAttributeName": "Watering",
"dataFormat": "CSV",
"dataFileContainsHeader": true,
"attributes": [
   {
     "attributeName": "Temperature",
     "attributeType": "NUMERIC"
   },
   {
     "attributeName": "Humidity",
     "attributeType": "NUMERIC"
   },
```

```
  {
    "attributeName": "Watering",
    "attributeType": "Categorical"
  }
 ]
}
```

The next step is to upload the data and schema files into Amazon S3. Currently, Amazon Machine Learning can work with data from Amazon S3 and Amazon Redshift. For demo, we use Amazon S3 to store data and schema files.

Now you can upload the `Temp-Hum-Water.csv` and `Temp-Hum-Water.csv.schema` files into Amazon S3. You can see my data in the following screenshot:

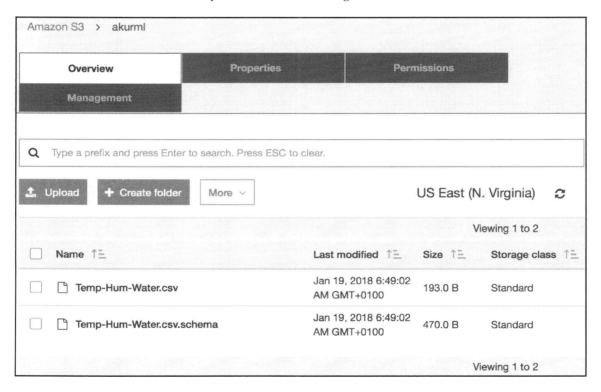

We will build a machine learning model from Amazon Machine Learning in the next section.

Building a machine learning model

This section will show how to build a model using Amazon Machine Learning. You can open the browser and navigate to `https://console.aws.amazon.com/machinelearning`. Proceed with the following steps:

1. You can create a model by clicking on the `Launch` button. If you never created a model, you can see it in the following screenshot. Otherwise, you can create a model from the menu in the Amazon Machine Learning dashboard:

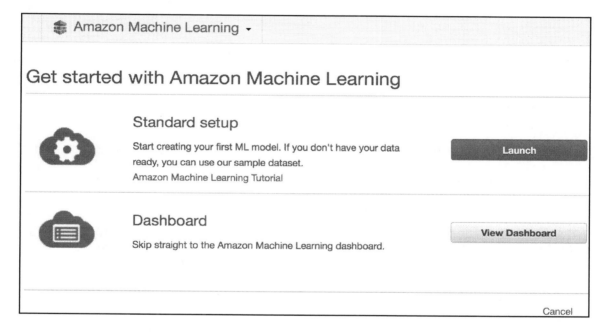

You should get a screen that is shown in the following screenshot. Fill the **S3 location** field from our data file:

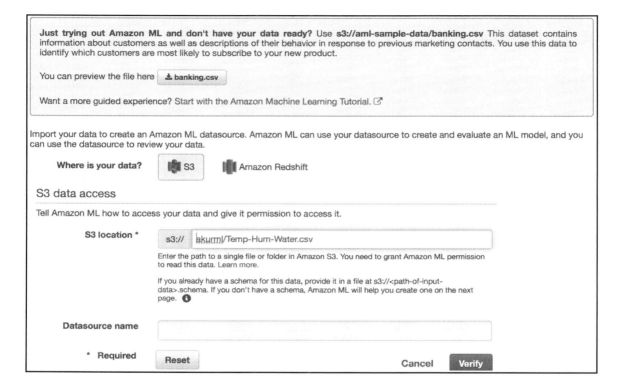

2. Next, click on the **Verify** button to check our data and schema validity. If successful, you should get a confirmation that is shown in the following screenshot:

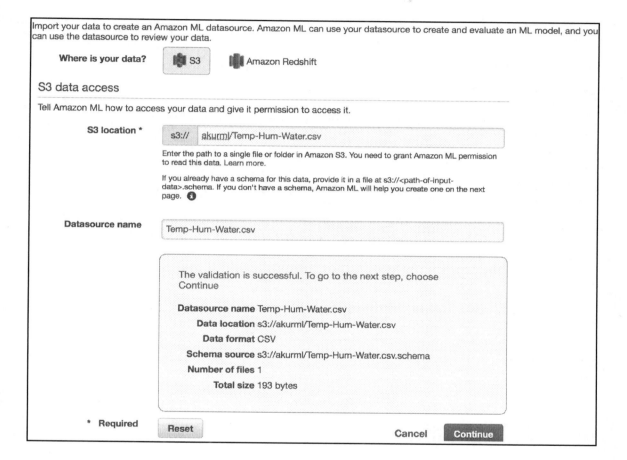

Import your data to create an Amazon ML datasource. Amazon ML can use your datasource to create and evaluate an ML model, and you can use the datasource to review your data.

Where is your data?   S3   Amazon Redshift

S3 data access

Tell Amazon ML how to access your data and give it permission to access it.

S3 location *   s3://   akurml/Temp-Hum-Water.csv

Enter the path to a single file or folder in Amazon S3. You need to grant Amazon ML permission to read this data. Learn more.

If you already have a schema for this data, provide it in a file at s3://<path-of-input-data>.schema. If you don't have a schema, Amazon ML will help you create one on the next page.

Datasource name   Temp-Hum-Water.csv

The validation is successful. To go to the next step, choose Continue

Datasource name Temp-Hum-Water.csv

Data location s3://akurml/Temp-Hum-Water.csv

Data format CSV

Schema source s3://akurml/Temp-Hum-Water.csv.schema

Number of files 1

Total size 193 bytes

* Required   Reset   Cancel   Continue

3. Click on the **Continue** button, and you should see the schema. You can modify the schema if you feel that it is not correct. Click on the **Continue** button once you finish:

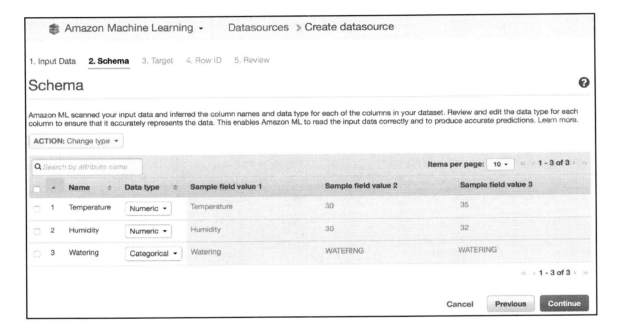

4. In the next step, you will select the target. By default, the `Watering` column will be set as the target column. In the **Row ID** section, we don't set anything. Now you can verify all input data settings in the **Review** section. You can see my input data settings in the following screenshot:

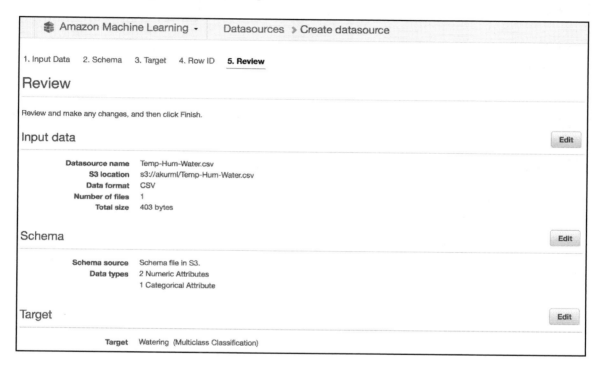

5. Next, we configure the machine learning model. Amazon Machine Learning will use multiclass for the model type that is shown in the following screenshot:

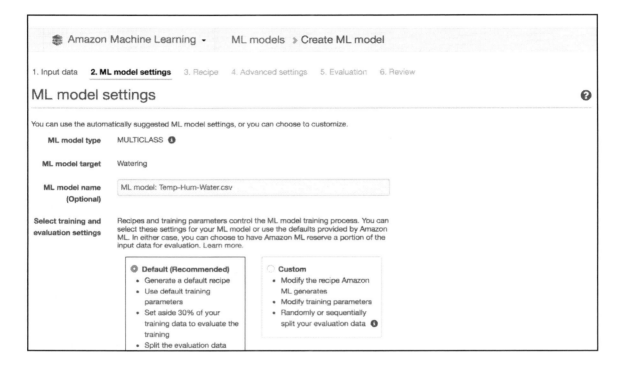

6. You can use default settings until the **Review** section. You can see my ML model in the following screenshot:

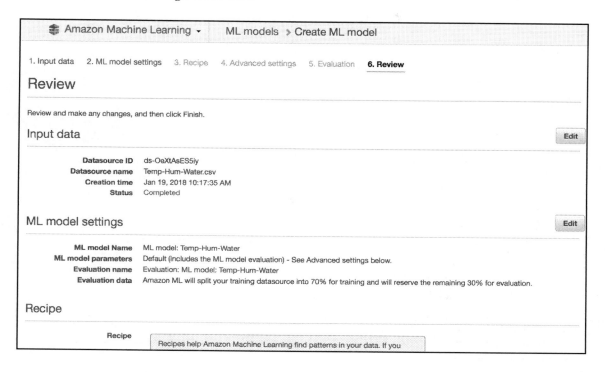

7. Amazon Machine Learning will create the model. Wait until all tasks are completed. You can see my model in the following screenshot:

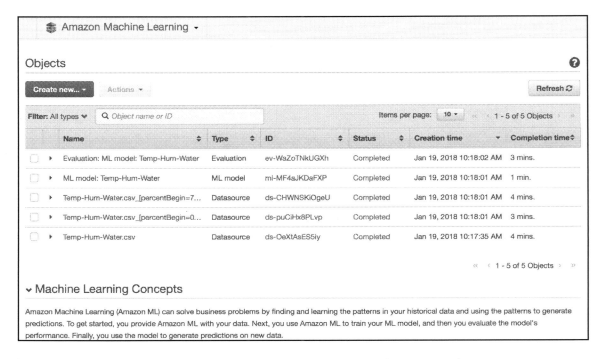

After all tasks are completed, you can verify and make predictions. In the next section, we will work towards making a prediction.

Evaluating and testing the model

Proceed with the steps as follows:

1. You can click your model evaluation from the Amazon Machine Learning dashboard. After clicking, you should get a screen, as shown in the following screenshot. If you find a wrong result, you should modify the data and then create a model:

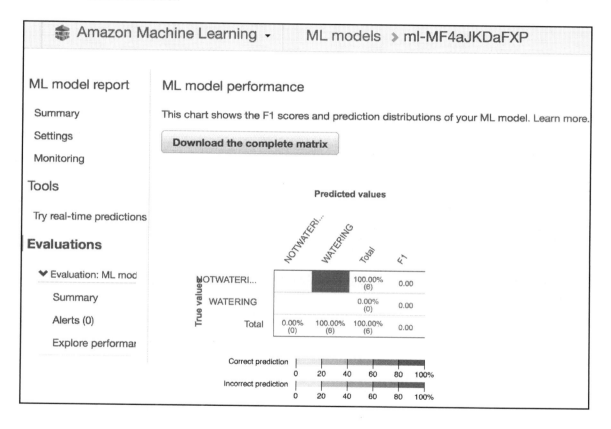

2. You can scroll down to see the **Predictions** section. You can perform testing by clicking on the **Try real-time predictions** button:

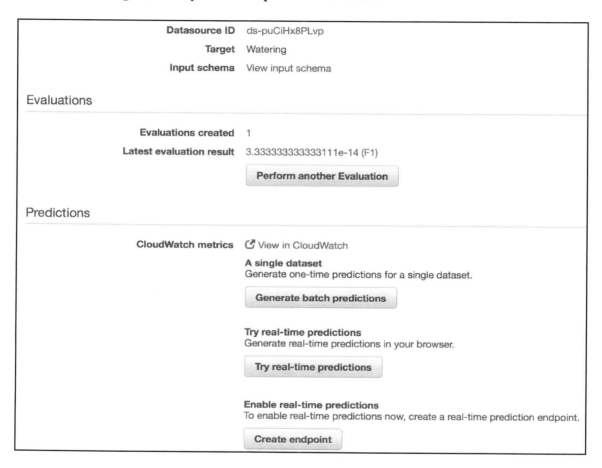

3. Then, you should have the **Try real-time predictions** screen. Now fill in the temperature and humidity values. After this, click on the **Create prediction** button. You should see a result in JSON format. A sample of program output can be seen in the following screenshot:

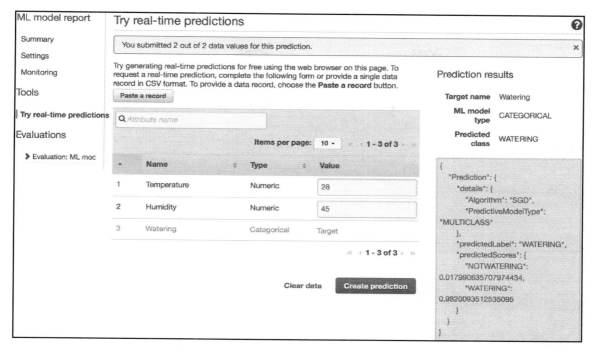

You have learned how to build a machine learning model and make a prediction. You can practice more by implementing AWS Lambda to consume AWS Machine Learning, so your application can consume this engine, for instance, Node.js, Python in computer or Raspberry Pi.

Summary

You learned several AWS Machine Learning services, such as Amazon Polly, Amazon Alexa, and Amazon Rekognition. Then, you also learned to build predictive analytics for IoT data.

In the next chapter, you will learn about AWS IoT security.

8
Securing AWS IoT

Our IoT devices and data are important assets, and we want to protect these assets from bad guys. In this chapter, we will explore the security aspects of IoT platforms in general and AWS IoT in particular.

We will explore the following topics in this chapter:

- Introducing IoT security
- Understanding IoT risks
- Introducing AWS IoT identity and security
- Securing communication between AWS IoT and IoT devices
- Authenticating and authorizing
- Managing AWS IAM
- Building a secure AWS IoT for your IoT project

Introducing IoT security

Security is one of the most important aspects in IT. In general, if we discuss security, we can say that all security stuff can be applied to any case. In the context of IoT, we also can enforce common security keys in an IoT environment.

There are a lot of security challenges in IoT. The following is a list of some of them:

- Secure IoT devices
- Authorizing and authenticating devices
- Managing device updates
- Securing communication
- Ensuring data privacy and integrity
- Detecting vulnerabilities and incidents

Some IoT devices have their own security guidelines from their principles to harden their security issues. In this chapter, we focus on IoT security focussing on AWS IoT. Some security challenges will be addressed in this chapter.

Understanding IoT risks

Understanding your project's implementation is crucial to understanding the security risks associated with it. When you decide on an architecture solution for your project, you should understand the pros and cons from your solution. In the security context, if you understand your IoT projects risks, you will be aware of potential threats to your project. One of the potential risks is security. When we talk about security risk, we are talking about security threats. Security threats can originate from two primary sources—humans and nature.

You can find a list of common security threats for IT in general. One of the resources is https://www.getcybersafe.gc.ca/cnt/rsks/cmmn-thrts-en.aspx. Some security books also provide security threat index for IT.

After we have identified security threats, we can mitigate the findings. To perform mitigation, it probably requires stakeholders to address the issue. Mitigation from threats should be validated in order to be sure of getting the best result. This workflow is depicted in the following figure:

Next, you should perform the threat modeling from the preceding figure based on your IoT projects.

Introducing AWS IoT identity and security

Consider that you have an office in a certain city. You have special assets within the office, so you don't allow people to come without your permission. Each person that comes to your office you will ask about their identity and purpose. If you feel that they have a vague identity, you can prevent them from coming to your office. This situation can be applied in AWS IoT.

Amazon AWS IoT applies identity and security to all IoT devices that want to access AWS IoT resources. All IoT devices should be registered to AWS IoT Management Console. You can perform this task using a browser and navigating to `https://console.aws.amazon.com/iot`. In the **Manage** section in the left-hand menu, you can add your IoT devices. You can see the AWS IoT Management Console in the following screenshot. AWS will charge based on the number of registered IoT devices:

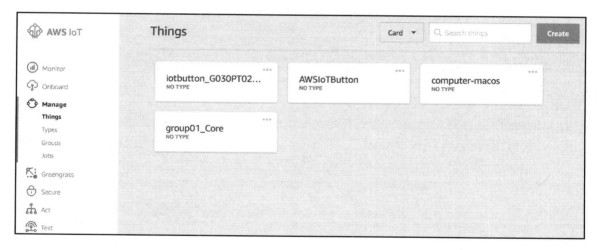

The task of registering IoT devices has already been covered in `Chapter 1`, *Getting Started with AWS IoT,* and you can read and review it. The result of registration is getting an AWS IoT device certificate. It consists of certificate and key files.

You also can register IoT devices using the command line through AWS CLI. You can use the `create-keys-and-certificate` command. Please read how to use it on `https://docs.aws.amazon.com/cli/latest/reference/iot/create-keys-and-certificate.html`. To perform this task, you should install AWS CLI. You can read the installation instructions for AWS CLI at `https://github.com/aws/aws-cli`.

Each IoT device will have its own security certificate. When you register a new IoT device, AWS IoT will generate a security certificate for your IoT device. AWS also provides a custom security certificate. You can bring your own security certificate and then upload it to AWS IoT.

If you want to use your own security certificate, you can create a new certificate from the AWS IoT Management Console. Proceed with the following steps:

1. You can select the **Use my certificate** option by clicking on the **Get started** button, as shown in the following screenshot:

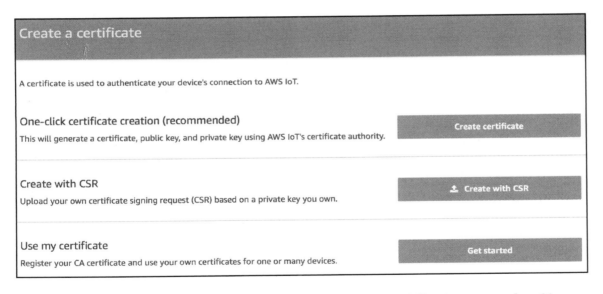

2. Next, you should see the screen that is shown in the following screenshot. You can click on the **Register CA** button to create a new security certificate:

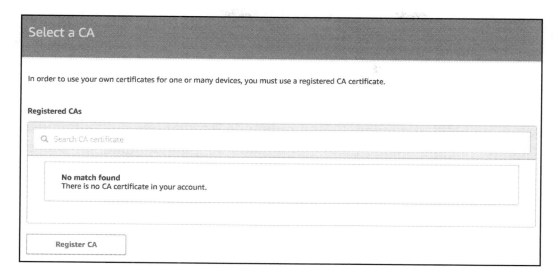

3. The next screen shows some steps to generate a certificate using `openssl`. Complete these steps to generate a certificate file that you can upload to AWS IoT:

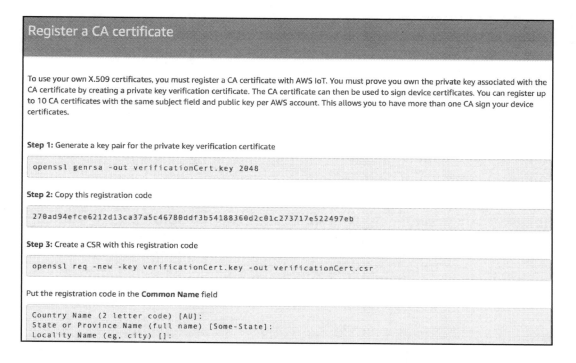

After performing these steps, you can use own security certificate on AWS IoT. You probably can attach your own security certificate file for all IoT devices.

Securing communication between AWS IoT and IoT devices

We need to have a secure communication between IoT device and AWS IoT. To achieve this goal, AWS IoT applies a security certificate as a part of securing communication. When we register a new IoT device, we also provide a security certificate file that is generated by AWS IoT or upload our own security certificate.

Since AWS IoT uses a security certificate, our IoT devices should support this feature. Ensure that your IoT device supports SSL certificates. Arduino Yún and Raspberry Pi 3 are examples of IoT devices with a supported SSL certificate. This certificate file should be uploaded to your IoT device.

Each IoT device has its own guidelines to upload a security certificate file. For Arduino Yún and Raspberry Pi 3, you can read how to work with AWS IoT in `Chapter 2`, *Connecting IoT Devices to AWS IoT Platform*.

Authentication and authorization

You have learned how to set up identity and secure communication for IoT devices. When an IoT device with its identity accesses AWS IoT, this IoT device will be challenged to verify its access rights.

To verify access rights for an IoT device, we can apply for **authentication** and **authorization**. Authentication is the process of verifying who you are. Authorization is the process of verifying that you have access to something.

Because we have applied an identity to our IoT device and registered it to AWS IoT, we are done with authentication. We will know the IoT device's identity, that accesses AWS IoT. When IoT device accesses AWS IoT resources without identity registration to AWS IoT, it will be rejected by AWS IoT.

Authorization in AWS IoT can be done through the AWS IoT policy. We can apply a policy to each IoT device. When you register a new IoT device, this will generate a security certificate and its policy. You can find a list of AWS IoT policies in the left-hand menu; go to **Secure| Policies**, as shown in the following screenshot:

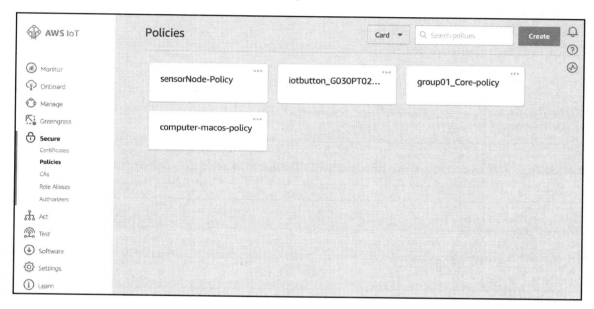

Technically, it is in JSON format that consists of access rights from its policy. For instance, you can see the following policy example. To see the policy setting, you can edit your policy on the AWS IoT policies dashboard. You can see a list of access rights in the `Statement[]` for each resource. For AWS IoT, an access right can be `iot:Publish`, `iot:Subscribe`, `iot:Connect`, and `iot:Receive`:

```
{
    "Version": "2012-10-17",
    "Statement": [
     {
      "Effect": "Allow",
      "Action": "iot:Publish",
      "Resource": "arn:aws:iot:<aws-iot-host>:topic/replaceWithATopic"
     },
     {
      "Effect": "Allow",
      "Action": "iot:Subscribe",
      "Resource": "arn:aws:iot:<aws-iot-
host>:topicfilter/replaceWithATopicFilter"
```

```
    },
    {
      "Effect": "Allow",
      "Action": "iot:Connect",
      "Resource": "arn:aws:iot:<aws-iot-
host>:client/replaceWithAClientId"
    },
    {
      "Effect": "Allow",
      "Action": "iot:Receive",
      "Resource": "arn:aws:iot:<aws-iot-host>:topic/replaceWithATopic"
    }
  ]
}
```

When you add a new policy, you will be asked for some actions, shown in the following screenshot. You can type any action depending on your needs. You should minimize security access for the IoT device. This is important for addressing security issues:

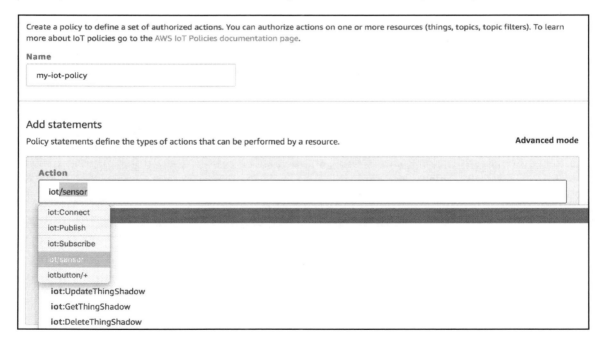

Finally, you should investigate your all IoT devices and their needs. Configuring less access from IoT devices can harden your system security.

Managing AWS IAM

AWS **Identity and Access Management** (**IAM**) is one of the Amazon services for managing your identity and access rights on any AWS resource. You can manage users, roles, and policies. You can find the AWS IAM Management Console at `https://console.aws.amazon.com/iam/`.

AWS provides IAM for managing all resource security and policies. Through AWS IAM, we can control and limit access and permission for any resource. You can create a new user and set its permission. For security reasons, you should investigate the user's need. You should set minimum permission to access AWS resources. Remove resource permissions if the user does not need them. You can see user permissions on the **Permissions** tab, as shown in the following screenshot:

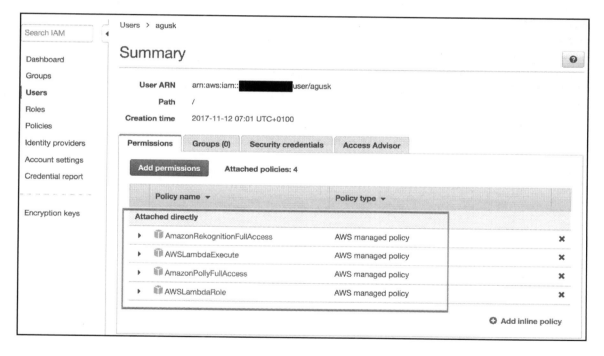

As a best security practice, you should not use a user account to access resources directly. You can create an access key ID to access those resources. You can see an access key list in the following screenshot. In this case, you should review access keys for all users to see whether those access keys are still used or not. If an access key ID is not used, you should remove it:

Next, we review our roles on AWS IAM. When we create AWS Lambda, we will set a role on that Lambda. This role is applied to resource permissions. All the security roles on AWS can found in the **Roles** submenu in AWS IAM. For instance, open one of the roles. You can see a list of policies attached to that role. You can see this in the following screenshot:

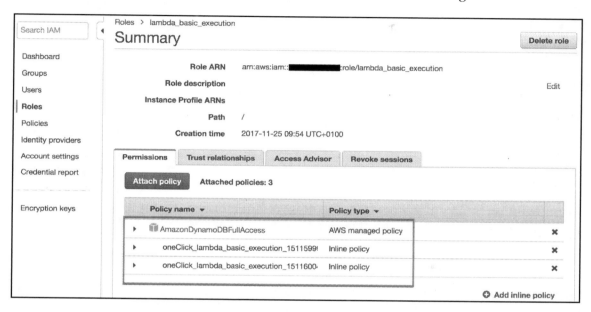

In this case, you should review each role. If you find roles that are not used on your system, you should remove them. Furthermore, you should review policy usage attached to that role. Remove policies if the role does not need them.

AWS IAM also provides the ability to create a custom policy. You can create a new policy with specific permissions on certain resources, as shown in the following screenshot. You can set the Amazon services that will be attached to the policy included in the **Actions** permission:

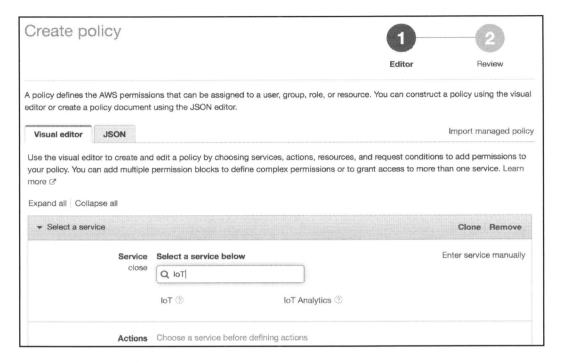

Finally, you should perform a security audit on AWS IAM regularly, for instance, every month. This action can increase the security level of your system.

Building a secure AWS IoT for your IoT project

An IoT project can be treated as an IT project in general. You should think of security issues when you implement an IoT project. Security specifications should be prepared during the first stage of the IoT project. People usually think about security aspects after a system has been built. The disadvantage of this approach is that we probably need to change more features in the design and implementation of the IoT project.

In this section, we will review some of the actions related to security views. You have probably implemented these security actions in your IoT projects.

Designing and implementing

When you design an IoT project, you should also think about security features in your IoT project. Security features can enforce security in an IoT project. The following are some security features that could be implemented in your IoT projects:

- Securing IoT devices
- Supporting a secure protocol such as TLS/SSL
- Secure gateway

IoT device should be designed in order to support secure protocol. Some MCU chips support secure protocols such as TLS/SSL. You can select one of those chips in your IoT device design.

Sometimes, IoT devices connect to a server through the internet. This operation usually needs a gateway. In this scenario, you should perform a secure gateway to ensure secure communication between the IoT devices and the server.

Performing regular security testing

Security in science and technology are changing fast, and we should be aware of this situation. In the context of the IoT projects, you should perform regular security testing. The objective of security testing is to ensure that IoT system is secure.

You can perform security testing all by yourself with the help of your team, or you also can hire a professional security consultant to perform security testing.

Working with security best practices

Making a secure system is hard, but you learn from other people how to build a secure system. This is usually named security best practices. This consists of recommendations for security actions. I recommend you read AWS documents about security at `https://aws.amazon.com/security/security-resources/`. You also can read security best practices for AWS at `https://aws.amazon.com/whitepapers/aws-security-best-practices/`.

Summary

You have learned the basics of IoT security. We have reviewed some aspects of IoT security. We have also explored security features of AWS IoT. Finally, we reviewed how to use AWS IAM to harden IoT projects.

Other Books You May Enjoy

If you enjoyed this book, you may be interested in these other books by Packt:

Azure IoT Development Cookbook
Yatish Patil

ISBN: 978-1-78728-300-8

- Build IoT Solutions using Azure IoT & Services
- Learn device configuration and communication protocols
- Understand IoT Suite and Pre-configured solutions
- Manage Secure Device communications
- Understand Device management, alerts
- Introduction with IoT Analytics, reference IoT Architectures
- Reference Architectures from Industry
- Pre-Configured IoT Suite solutions

MQTT Essentials - A Lightweight IoT Protocol
Gastón C. Hillar

ISBN: 978-1-78728-781-5

- Understand how MQTTv3.1 and v3.1.1 works in detail
- Install and secure a Mosquitto MQTT broker by following best practices
- Design and develop IoT solutions combined with mobile and web apps that use MQTT messages to communicate
- Explore the features included in MQTT for IoT and Machine-to-Machine communications
- Publish and receive MQTT messages with Python, Java, Swift, JavaScript, and Node.js
- Implement the security best practices while setting up the MQTT Mosquitto broker

Leave a review - let other readers know what you think

Please share your thoughts on this book with others by leaving a review on the site that you bought it from. If you purchased the book from Amazon, please leave us an honest review on this book's Amazon page. This is vital so that other potential readers can see and use your unbiased opinion to make purchasing decisions, we can understand what our customers think about our products, and our authors can see your feedback on the title that they have worked with Packt to create. It will only take a few minutes of your time, but is valuable to other potential customers, our authors, and Packt. Thank you!

Index

Made in the USA
Middletown, DE
17 May 2019